May your interest in the
fragile art of Ikebana
continue and grow.
        Sincerely
            Lida Webb

Popular Styles of

Japanese Flower Arrangement

Popular Styles of
Japanese Flower Arrangement

By Lida Webb

Drawings by Larry Keith

Hearthside Press Incorporated

Publishers   New York

Contents

Dedicated
to my
husband
who shares my love of flowers

Author's note

This book is written to answer the need for information on the various styles of Japanese flower arrangement, arising from an unprecedented upsurge of interest in things Oriental. Interior decorators, architects, furniture designers, and landscape gardeners seem suddenly to have found in the Japanese art forms a simplicity and beauty which fit contemporary needs.

This enthusiasm will not surprise the American flower arranger, who has long known that with three flowers or branches the Japanese can create designs of compelling beauty. In fact, flower arrangement books originating in Japan have been popular here for many years.

Most of the books dealt in their turn with only *one* of the many styles of Oriental floral design. There are many, many styles . . . all deservedly popular in the country of their origin . . . and all of them challenging enough to be known here. My interest in the many neglected facets of Japanese arrangement and especially in correlating the information offered by different masters led to this book.

Appreciation

Some months ago I prepared but did not distribute a pamphlet on judging Japanese flower arrangements, with the sole idea of assisting judges and exhibitors to evaluate and create arrangements in the Japanese manner. It was my good fortune to be able to discuss the material with Mrs. Tomoko Yamamoto of Des Moines, Iowa. She encouraged me to release it, with the suggestion, however, that it be enlarged.

Later, I consulted Mrs. Emma Hodkinson Cyphers of Clifton, New Jersey, for whose intelligence and store of knowledge I have the most profound respect and who, over a period of years, has been most gracious in helping me to reconcile seemingly insoluble problems. Mrs. Cyphers felt that the book should be developed to deal with specific schools of Japanese floral art whose flower forms would be most adaptable to Western living, and thus produce a work that would be of interest to the average homemaker. I am deeply indebted to Mrs. Cyphers for her patience and helpful suggestions throughout the preparation of this text.

To my Japanese teacher of many years, Mrs. S. Arai of Houston, Texas, I express my sincere gratitude for introducing me to Japanese flower arranging, and for patiently training and counselling me through the ensuing years.

By no means least of the many friends to whom I feel humbly indebted is Mrs. John R. Salois of Dallas, who served as Texas Flower Show School Chairman, and later as National Flower Show School Chairman. Under her I took my first course in the Flower Show School, and it was she who many years later suggested that I prepare myself to teach. There has never been an occasion when I have sought her counsel or advice, that she has not wholeheartedly extended it.

Some of the many widely followed Japanese schools were omitted from this text because information concerning their methods was unavailable. It is my hope, however, that you will find enough inspiration here to pursue the study of Japanese floral art.

Lida Webb

Popular Styles of

Japanese Flower Arrangement

CHAPTER I

THE ART AND TECHNIQUE OF IKEBANA

To better understand and more deeply appreciate their floral art, one must realize that to the Japanese people arranging flowers is a way of life, filled with spiritual and philosophical connotations. Westerners love flowers for their physical beauty, but the Orientals consider them a part of the universal truth by which one achieves wisdom and composure. This philosophy imbues the teaching of every master of the Japanese floral art.

The word *Ikebana* has its English equivalent in the term "flower arrangement" but implicit in the original Japanese meaning was such placement of flowers in a vessel as to most strikingly reveal their finest characteristics. For this reason, I can suggest no better beginning for anyone interested in Japanese arrangements than a walk or a drive where one may observe natural plant growth. Perhaps you will be rewarded, as I frequently am, by finding a few branches which curve naturally into the form you want. But the real reward comes as you observe flowers (the term includes all growing plants) and their habits, applying what you see to making Japanese-style arrangements, for fidelity to nature is typical of *Ikebana*, except for the deliberate distortions sometimes practiced in certain classical designs.

Ikebana is not only an abstract philosophy, but it can also be used for decoration, felicitation, and for personal pleasure. In many respects, Westerners and Orientals use flowers in similar ways.

For instance, in Japan, one class of *Ikebana* is practiced for ceremonial and religious observances, analogous to our church arrangements. Medicinal herbs or flowers symbolizing good omens are used as expressions of congratulation. Similarly we send flowers to new mothers, and to friends on anniversaries and birthdays. Flowers are also used to transmit moral lessons, but here the parallel ends, because I fear that we Americans have not progressed to the point where we can either write or read a floral message of moral significance!

The second class of *Ikebana* consists of arrangements for decoration, similar to our own procedure of using flowers to fit the place and occasion.

In the third class of *Ikebana*, arrangements made solely for pleasure, there is no restriction as to the kinds of flowers used. So too, here in America, many of our best interpretive arrangements are unrestricted as to plant material.

DESIGN ELEMENTS

The Japanese people have a strong predilection for line, regarding it as more expressive than any other form. This affinity for line is apparent in the architecture of the country, its landscaping, and in the raiment of the people. Certainly, line is indisputably the most important element in any Japanese flower arrangement.

Line forms are important, too. Straight lines are forceful and strong, rigid and unyielding; curved ones are more classical, and suggest femininity and gentleness.

The effectiveness, from a psychological standpoint, of line directions cannot be underestimated. While vertical and horizontal lines have a feeling of firmness and permanence, they are rigidly uncompromising and lack movement, whereas a slanting line, though unstable, does express motion.

A theory which is put into practice in modern Japanese flower arrangement, is that a line which reaches forward demands of the observer acknowledgment of its existence, while the line which slants backward is tranquil, unassuming and likely to go unnoticed (though its omission would be detrimental to the design.)

There is a special significance, too, in the number of lines used. One line, depending upon its shape and direction, is expressive and will react in specific ways upon the emotions; two or more lines, used with discrimination, will suggest harmony and development.

The form of any Japanese flower arrangement is fundamentally triangular and, if properly constructed, triangles within triangles will be found throughout the design. These are neither equilateral nor isosceles, but scalene triangles.

Texturally, wide latitude is possible. Plants which grow in the same environment can be combined for a flower arrangement. This fact precludes a slavish adherence by the Japanese artist to man-made rules relating to compatible textures. Nature herself deals in contrasts as well as harmonies, and it is from nature that the Japanese arranger seeks inspiration.

Color is not of major importance in Japanese floral art, and in the modern abstract style, it is used to accentuate form, rather than for its own sake. This is in contrast to the so-called European "period" arrangements, particularly the French ones, where line is subordinated to color.

SEASON AND TIME SYMBOLISM

In all forms of *Ikebana,* seasons are observed. In the early *Moribana* forms, seasons are denoted by the water level in the container. In Spring, the pan, vase or bowl is filled with water, and the amount is gradually reduced as the season advances. In present-day *Moribana,* the bowl is always filled with water and the seasons indicated by the *area* of water surface left exposed. For Winter arrangements, water is not visible at all, the entire surface being covered with small, tight bunches of cypress, lycopodium or other long-lived plant which will not become discolored in nor foul the water. With the advancing season, the amount of greens (club moss in Japan) is reduced and the water surface increased. The relative areas of greens and water are indicative of the season.

Seasons are likewise represented, in most methods, by the stage of development of the plants used. In Spring, young green growth is indicated. In summer, full-blown flowers in profusion are used. In Fall, dried materials and leaves which have turned from green to the russet tones, are appropriate; and in Winter, proper materials are either stark, unadorned branches, or evergreens, frequently combined with berries or camellias to exude warmth. In the *Koriu* Method of the *Enshui-ryu,* there was a rule that Earth, representing the Present, must always be of green material.

Plants are used to suggest time too. For instance, buds represent the future, perfect leaves and partly open blossoms symbolize the present, and dried materials or flowers in full bloom signify the past.

Since many of the flowers used by the Japanese may not be available to us, for one reason or another, it seems to me sensible and sufficient, in creating flower arrangements in their manner, to combine flowers which grow seasonally in the same habitat and in accord with their characteristics of growth. As an example: we use small flowers and buds in the top and outer edges of the design, but in Japanese-style arrangements we should use the iris high because it naturally grows taller than the lily-of-the-valley.

PLANT SYMBOLISM

To the Orientals, flowers may be a means of communicating sentimental, spiritual, reverential or congratulatory messages. The language of flowers, of course, is not universally spoken, and an arrangement which might be clear to a native Japanese would probably be unintelligible to the average Westerner. A few of the most popular flowers and their meanings are listed below:

bamboo—used for honesty

cherry—king of flowers. The blossom symbolizes knightly deportment, service, and sacrifice. No other flower may be shown in the room with cherry blossoms. May be combined only with pine

chrysanthemum—national flower of Japan. Called long-lasting plant because it grows throughout the four seasons. A reminder that life is transitory. Appropriate for any occasion and degree of formality or informality

iris—has high rank but purple iris is banned for weddings. In Japan purple is the color of mourning. Swordshaped leaves symbolize military courage. Believed to possess power to repel illness and evil; the white iris, with soft leaves is symbol of purity and suitable for all congratulatory occasions

lotus—when used alone, it represents the whole span of human life; sacred flower of Buddhism

maple—poison-dispelling plant, the belief being that it absorbs all undesirable elements

narcissus—appears during Winter and remains until Spring, so is the plant of two sexes. Symbolizes strength, valor, and chastity

peony—associated with the aristocratic in the Orient

pine—most popular in Japanese floral art. Represents vigor, long life, and also old age

plum—emblem of courage, perseverance, chastity, womanhood. (Pine, bamboo, and plum are frequently combined to celebrate births, marriages, and longevity)

willow and frog—symbolizes tenacity

wisteria—plant of two seasons because it blooms in Spring and Summer. White variety highly favored for congratulatory occasions. Violet variety is not used at weddings.

SEX SYMBOLISM

Female: Buds of flowers or blossoms past their prime. Blue, yellow and white colors. The back of the leaf is regarded as female. Large leaves, when used, are curved, bent or turned so that the "male" and "female" sides are shown alternately.

Male: The front of a leaf or flower. Flowers at their most vigorous stage. Red, violet, pink, and variegated flowers.

COLOR RANK

With few exceptions, the white flower of every species is ranked highest.

The yellow chrysanthemum ranks highest. Other flowers accorded first place in rank, according to species, are: Pale pink peach blossoms; yellow Kerria japonica (an exception since there is a white variety); purple iris; red camellia; pale violet wisteria (ranked above the white variety); red tree peony; light red peony albiflora; yellow valerian; red lespedeza; dark blue convolvulus; pale pink cherry blossom.

A rich green ranks first in color among leaves. Green leaves or white flowers are used for blending colors which are not harmonious. White, or other highest ranking color is used as most important placement when combined with other colors.

CONTAINERS

As in any arrangement regardless of origin, the container and floral material should be inherently compatible in shape, size, color, and texture. An extremely tall arrangement appears better balanced and more stable in a low container, and a horizontal arrangement is more effective in a taller vase. The drawings in this book will illustrate the point.

By covering a greater area of a too-long or too-large container with floral material, the visual force of the container can be reduced. In the case of a too-small container, its importance can be emphasized by leaving numerous open spaces in the design, thereby revealing more of the container.

Ikenobo arrangements are unsuitable for any but certain traditional containers. As various methods of *Ikenobo* arrangement were developed, containers were selected with as great care as were the plant materials, because the vase is considered an integral part of the composition.

A cylindrical bamboo or bronze vase is formal; any type of *usubata* is semi-formal; the boat, bamboo tube with two or more openings, hanging baskets, pitchers, and similar containers are informal.

Nageire and *Heika* arrangements are made in tall vases, baskets, pitchers, and similar articles while *Moribana* arrangements call for low, flat bowls. If the bowl has three legs only, it should be placed on a thin base so that the one leg will be at center front.

Since the resumption of trade between the United States and Japan, there has been a steady flow into this country of lovely old containers or their modern counterparts. Among the latter are Chinese lacquer vases in shapes suitable for arrangements in the Japanese manner.

Just as *Ikenobo* arrangements require traditional containers, so also do traditional Japanese containers demand classical *Ikenobo* arrangements. Modern Western-world designs are unsuitable in them.

BASES

Bases are usually placed beneath vases or bowls. Rectangular bases (either straight-sided or curved) are used under round or oval-shaped containers, and round or irregularly-shaped bases under square or rectangular vessels.

The Japanese use bases or flower stands for the same reasons American arrangers do:

1) For practical considerations, such as protecting surfaces against damage from water or scratches; providing a firm foundation on which to set the arrangement.

2) Because bases are in themselves decorative and may provide the necessary element to round out the shape of the arrangement; or to scale up a too-small design to make it appear larger.

3) An appropriate base, used as an integral part of the flower arrangement, will make of it a complete entity, independent of its decorative surroundings.

A bamboo container is never placed on a bamboo raft, nor is it appropriate to use bamboo branches in a bamboo vase. Baskets are never placed on stands.

CONTROLS

Different mechanics are required for constructing classical arrangements.

KUBARI (or MATAGI)

A *kubari*, (which some teachers call a *matagi*) is defined as a "Y-shaped wooden holder for a narrow-necked vase." Uusually, a forked branch is employed, cut to fit firmly inside the vase, the prongs of the fork placed about ¾ inch from the top of the vase, with the base about ½ inch inside the vase. As indicated, the *kubari* is positioned differently for the Formal, Semi-Formal and Informal Classical arrangements. (Figs. 1, 2, 3.)

After the fork is secured, the flowers are placed within it. Behind the stems or branches, a cross-piece, called *komi*, is fitted firmly into the vase to hold the materials in place. This cross-piece and the base of the fork should be the same distance from the top of the vase to prevent the branches from wobbling.

Considerable practice is needed in the use of the *kubari* but once the techniques have been mastered its advantages are fully apparent.

Dried woody material is best for the *kubari*, but it must be soaked

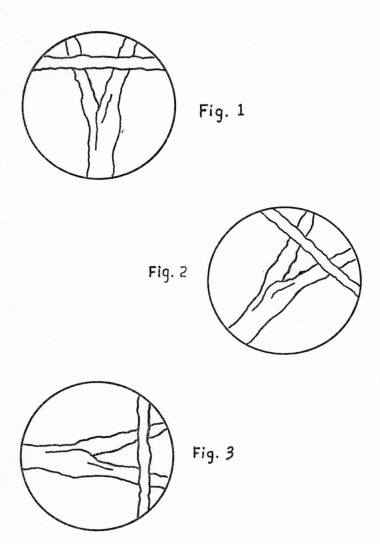

Kubari with komi, Ikenobo Classical Forms: Fig. 1, Formal; Fig. 2, Semi-Formal; Fig. 3, Informal.

in water for at least twenty-four hours before use; otherwise it could expand and break the vase.

One cannot always conveniently locate the proper-sized "fork" for the material at hand. In such case, a *kubari* can be made by taking two straight sticks, slightly longer than the diagonal of the vase, shaving one side of each at the end which will form the base of the fork, and wiring the two together. If very little is taken off the sticks the fork will be wide; the higher up the sticks are trimmed, and the more they are shaved, the narrower the fork will become. When "making" a *kubari*, do not fit it into the vase until after the trimming, wiring and soaking have been done, because altering the sticks and wiring them together will shorten the overall length.

CONTROLS FOR TALL VASES

The controls (sometimes called "fixtures") for holding materials in position in tall containers are similar for both *Nageire* and *Heika* arrangements. The arranger may improvise his own methods, dictated by the size, weight, shape and condition of the stems or branches.

The "split-branch" stay (Fig. 4) is used for either erect containers where the design is to be upright, or for jar-shaped containers. The stay, which may be either a straight stick or a forked one, is fitted to the inside walls of the vase by cutting the ends at a slant so they will hug the walls closely; then the branches are split and slightly spread so that they can be pressed down firmly over the stay. Branches should rest either on the bottom or the sides of the vase. If the arrangement is to take the upright position, the better method is for the stems to rest on the floor of the container; if the arrangement is to be slanting, then the stem ends must be cut at a slant which will rest securely against the side of the vase. There is no rule which forbids the use of tying materials, if additional traction is needed, to fasten the branches and stay together.

For the cylindrical vase, a cross-bar stay (Fig. 5) is most effective. The cross-bar is made by crossing two small sticks, tying them firmly together and inserting them in the vase about ½ inch from the opening. Lightweight branches may be placed to rest against the cross-bar at the point where the sticks are joined together, with

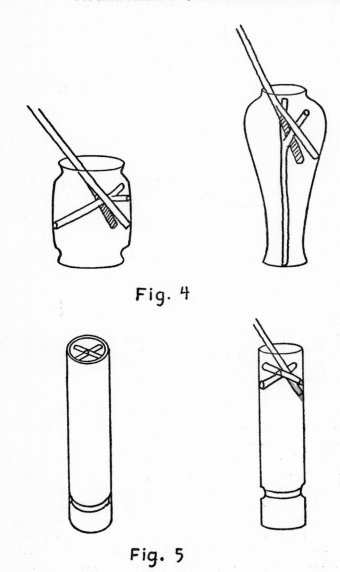

Fig. 4

Fig. 5

Controls for Nageire and Heika Forms: Fig. 4, Split-branch stay. Fig. 5, Cross-bar stay.

their ends cut at a slant to hug the inside wall of the vase; or, if the material is too heavy to stay in position without wiring, the branches can be secured to the crossbar at the point of intersection.

CONTROL FOR GLASS BOTTLE OR SMALL-NECKED VASE

In clear glass bottles or vases with small necks, it is often difficult to artistically arrange the stems below water. If you don't want the stems to show, a workable technique is to insert a fresh carrot in the opening, cut it off flush with the top of the vase, remove it and cut off the lower portion so that the carrot is about 1½ inch long; then ream out the center to a size which will accommodate all the stems to be used; thrust the stems (which have already been arranged in the hand) through the carrot, allowing only ¼ to ½ inch to extend beyond the lower opening, and insert the completed arrangement into the mouth of the vase. The "control" will fit snugly, the stems will rest in water, and the arrangement will have stability.

A turnip is serviceable as a fixture but not so easy to use. Irish potato is impractical because it dehydrates too quickly. The carrot or turnip will outlast the flowers.

The popular pin-point holder, called *kenzan,* is now almost universally used for Moribana arrangements, regardless of the method of teaching. It has supplanted many different and fanciful types of controls used in low bowls in the past.

The *kenzan* is *not* used in a tall vase.

CONTROLS FOR MORIBANA ARRANGEMENTS
GROOMING PLANT MATERIALS

Houn Ohara of the *Ohara-ryu* stresses the importance of pruning materials to give the best effects. He advocates thinning along the branch, leaving only the leaves or flowers near the tip. *(Fig. 6).* He also illustrates, in his demonstrations, how partial stripping of a branch will make it look longer. *(Fig. 7).*

According to Mr. Ohara, there is a right way and a wrong way to position flower heads. This is illustrated in *Fig. 8.*

In measuring lengths of stems used in an arrangement, his rule is that with a single flower at the tip the length is measured from just below the flower head. The stem of such material as gladiolus, stock, grasses, etc. is measured from the base of the stem to the point where the lowest floret, leaf or lateral appears on the stem. The length above the lowest floret is not considered in the measurement. *(Fig. 9.)*

In doing a natural scenery arrangement, using materials from the fields where they are subjected to the onslaught of high winds, Mr. Ohara says it is quite permissible to use a broken stem or branch, particularly that of a frail grass, and to let it extend horizontally through the arrangement. *(Fig. 10)*.

In doing a *Heika* arrangement in a tall vase, particularly one with a small mouth, it is sometimes easier to bend a stem and let it rest on the bottom of the vase, than it is to fit a stay into the container. If the bent portion of the stem is the width of the floor of the vase and rests securely on the bottom, the flower will stand erect. *(Fig. 11)*.

Some of the techniques mentioned are doubtless familiar to you; any of them, when needed, can facilitate the arranging of flowers.

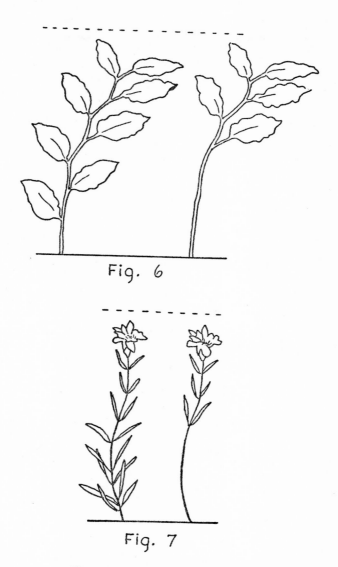

Fig. 6

Fig. 7

Figs. 6 and 7, Grooming Branches.

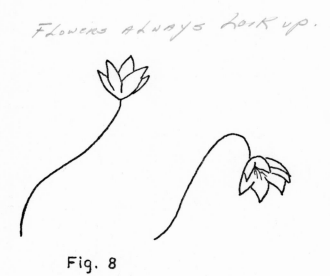

Fig. 8

Fig. 8, Right and wrong position of flower head.

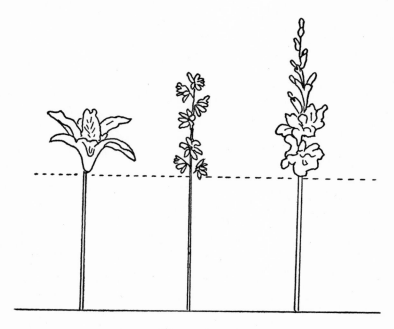

Fig. 9

Fig. 9, Stem measurements.

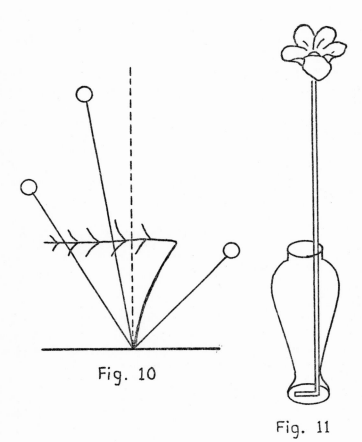

Fig. 10

Fig. 11

Fig. 10, Crossing Stem, Naturalistic Arrangement. Fig. 11, Bent Stem Control.

CHAPTER 2

THE IKENOBO SCHOOL

Japanese flower arrangement today shows an individualistic trend
—a free style—which departs almost completely from the sym-
bolisms of older schools. When this modern style is added to the
traditional styles which one must absorb, is it any wonder that the
Westerner becomes confused?

To minimize the confusion, I suggest that you begin by learning
something of the background and principles of the old Ikenobo
school on which, in one degree or another, all subsequent teachings
are based.

ITS ORIGIN

In the sixth century, scholars were sent to China to study the
literature, politics, religion and art of that country. One of the
emissaries, *Ono-no-Imoko*, was a Buddhist priest attached to the
Imperial Palace.

His report to the Prince Regent mentioned that the Buddhist
monks in China made offerings of growing plants to their gods,
and he expressed the conviction that the careless placing of plants
on the temple altars was unworthy of Buddha.

Ono-no-Imoko was commissioned to contrive a plan for arranging
flowers which would express both the spiritual and philosophical
precepts of Buddhism, whereupon he retired to a hut by a lake,
there to meditate upon the profound aspects of Life, Nature and
Religion.

History reveals that this scholar-priest spent the remainder of his
life, about fifty years, in concentrating upon the expression, through
plant materials, of the interdependence and import of the three great
rudiments of the universe—Heaven, Man and Earth—a precept of
the Buddhist religion.

RIKKWA

The oldest known form of flower arrangement in Japan, *Rikkwa*, a product of the early Ikenobo school, was designed for use in the Buddhist temples and to decorate the Imperial Court on formal occasions. It was developed to represent, in a composite grouping placed in one vase, the totality of existing or created things, including the earth (with all on or in it), the heavenly bodies and all else throughout space—in fact, all creation. The height of the plant material and container together averaged 5 feet, but often the dimensions were much greater. Due to its complexity and great size, the *Rikkwa* could never have been adapted to general use.

Ono-no-Imoka continued his experiments with growing plants, meditating on how their use would best symbolize the spirit of Buddha. In time, other priests sought instruction in his methods, and thus the *Ikenobo School* of flower arrangement developed. *Ikenobo* translated means "Hut by the Pond" or "Temple by the Lake," a reference to the founder's place of retirement.

IKENOBO GROWS

For a long time, *Ikebana* engaged only the priests and nobility, but in the fifteenth century, the Emperor Yoshimasa, patron of the arts, decreed that his subjects be taught flower arrangement as a means of developing their cultural life. It was during his reign too that the *tokonoma*—a recessed space designed for the display of a flower arrangement and other art objects—was introduced. This alcove helped promote flower arrangement to persons in all classes. Usually a scroll or *kakemono* was placed on the back wall of the *tokonoma*, and the flower arrangement was designed to emphasize the message painted on the scroll. The art of *Ikebana* continued to grow during the succeeding generations.

In the seventeenth century, when *Ikebana* had reached the peak of its classical beauty, certain rules were promulgated for attaining balance without symmetry. Measurements of the three main lines in *Ikenobo* arrangements have varied through the years, but these ancient rules for asymmetrical balance (which are recommended as a sound foundation for the study of any phase of Japanese floral art) were:

1) That the measurement of the tallest placement be at least 1½ times the height or width of the container.
2) That the tip of the tallest placement (Heaven) be directly above the point of emergence from the container.
3) That man be 2/3 the height of Heaven; Earth, 2/3 the height of man.
4) That all lines be held together at the base (forming *Nemoto*) for 2 to 3 inches above the water line.
5) That all lines point toward Heaven.

FORMS OF IKENOBO

The three forms of the older classical *Ikenobo* arrangement are the *Formal,* the *Semi-formal* and the *Informal.* These forms are, with the exception of slight differences in measurements, much the same as the classical *Ikenobo* taught by succeeding masters of Japanese flower arrangement.

GUIDING PRINCIPLES IN IKENOBO ARRANGEMENTS

In whatever form the *Ikenobo* arrangement may be, the Heaven placement always determines the proportions of the Man and Earth lines. The number of attributes, or supporting lines, added to each of the three main lines, depends upon both the quantity and size of the foliage and/or flowers on each branch, if foliage and/or flowers are present.

Slender, weak tips are disregarded, only the strongest part of the branch being measured.

Flowers and foliage, if any, should lie along the upper sides of the Man and Earth placements, with no drooping ornamentation on the undersides.

The disparity in length of branches should be the same in each grouping (Heaven group, Man group, Earth group). The attribute behind any main line must be longer than the one in front of the same main line.

The Man and Earth placements are lower than the Heaven branch in an *Ikenobo* arrangement. Any supporting lines added to these placements must be *between* the Man and Earth main branches and the Heaven branch.

Branches are held together for a distance of 3½ or more inches above the water level, to suggest a strong feeling of growth at the base of the arrangement. This union of stems is called *nemoto*.

As a rule, the classical arrangement consists of more than three lines. There are no set rules for the exact number of attributes to be used with any main branch. Material may be chosen which has branches growing from the main branch, or the illusion of such additional branches can be accomplished by adding pieces of shrubbery in such a manner that they appear as parts of the main branches.

Classical arrangements are restrained. They usually consist of one —certainly no more than two—kinds of plant material. Three kinds are combined only when two arrangements are made in a traditional bamboo vase with two openings. The relative curves of the main lines in *Ikenobo* arrangements of the classical form are much the same regardless of the school involved.

The *Formal Ikenobo* is always slender. The Heaven line curves above the *nemoto* and then returns to a position which places the tip directly over its base. The line arches to a rear corner of the receptacle, but does not extend beyond the limits of the vase.

The Man main line follows the Heaven line for a distance above the *Nemoto*, then flares outward with the tip turned back toward Heaven. The tip of this line extends beyond the extremity of the vase.

Earth is placed diagonally opposite Man, on the other side of Heaven, and its tip likewise is upturned toward Heaven.

The more the Heaven line curves, the less formal is the *Ikenobo* classical arrangement.

ENSHUI-RYU

One of the developments of *Ikenobo* was *Enshui-ryu*. It has been criticized by some as bizarre, while others have praised it as unique. The method known as *Koriu* is a product of the *Enshui-Ryu*.

The principal placements of the *Enshui-ryu* method are *Shin*, (Heaven), *So* (Man) and *Gyo* (Earth). The measurements are:

Heaven (*Shin*) —Height determined by placement. Due to exaggerated bow of this line, a definite height seems never to have been established.

Man (*So*) —About ½ of Heaven, with tip extending straight up.

Earth (*Gyo*) —¼ of Heaven.

The Heaven line is bent boldly sideways from a point a few inches above the *nemoto,* curving back to bring the tip directly above its base in order to maintain its center of gravity. The distinguishing feature of the *Enshui-ryu* method is the bold curvature of the Heaven line, which resembles a bow when strung.

Trailing plant materials, shaped into fantastic curves, may be used on either side of Heaven (the Man side or the Earth side), but not on both sides.

The artistic artificiality of this method requires painstaking manipulation of the branches. They must be softened and, with infinite patience, either bent or wired into shape and left for many hours until the curves become set. Regardless of liberties taken in the degree of curvature of the respective main branches, the tip of Heaven is always above its base.

Even in the double-opening bamboo cylinder, the lines take exaggerated curves, giving an impression of dominance in width over height of the arranged branches. Figure 12 illustrates the *Enshui-ryu* classical form.

Seasonal symbolism is observed, as it is in all Japanese schools. Spring arrangements are simple, yet potent in line and feeling, suggesting early and promising vegetation. A full, spreading arrangement is typical of summer, while that of autumn is sparse and lacking in fullness. The winter arrangement is faded and lifeless.

Dedicated students of Japanese floral art will find the *Enshui-ryu* method fascinating and a challenge to their artistic aspirations.

The *Koriu* method, whose origin is traced directly to the *Enshui-ryu,* bears a greater resemblance to the classical forms of *Ikenobo, Misho* and other schools which teach the classical styles.

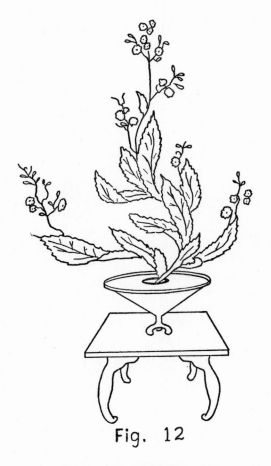

Fig. 12

Fig. 12, Enshui-ryu Classical Form.

SHOKA METHOD

Shoka (also spelled *Shokwa*), a method of arrangement emanating from the *Ikenobo* School, is still being taught in Japan. It is far less complex than *Rikkwa*, greatly reduced in size, and is appropriate for average home use.

CARDINAL PLACEMENTS

The measurements of the three principal placements in present-day *Shoka* are:

Heaven —1½ to 3 times the height of the container.
(*Shin*)
Man —about 2/3 the height of Heaven.
(*Soe*)
Earth —approximately 1/3 the height of Heaven.
(*Tai*)

BASIC FORMS

The fundamental forms of *Shoka* are the Formal (called *Shin*), *Fig. 13*, the Semi-formal (known as *Gyo*) *Fig. 14*, and the Informal (designated *So*) *Fig. 15*.

DOUBLE SHOKA

The double *Shoka* arrangement, done in a bamboo container with two openings, does not accommodate itself to any other type of container. Tree or shrub branches are used for the upper section, while flowers are required for the lower one; or, flowers of two different species may be used in the upper and lower sections, respectively.

The old *Ikenobo* rule of keeping the Heaven-Man-Earth combination as a single unit for some distance above the rim of the container, applies to both upper and lower arrangements. A *nejime* (in place of Earth) may be used in the upper arrangement, if desired, *Fig. 16*.

MISHO-RYU

The *Misho* School was founded by Mishosai Koho during the Bunsei Period (1818-1830). It remains one of the most popular schools of flower arrangement in Japan, its present Master (1958)

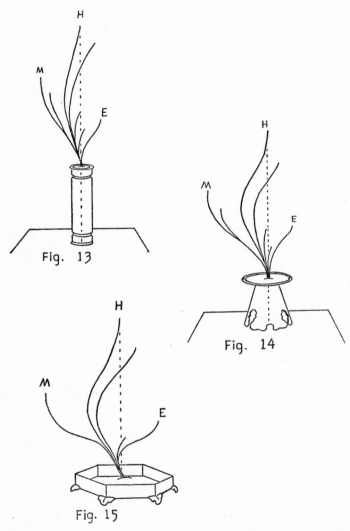

Fig. 13

Fig. 14

Fig. 15

Shoka Forms: Fig. 13, Formal (Shin). Fig. 14, Semi-Formal (Gyo). Fig. 15, Informal (So).

being Hein Koshu Tsujii, who holds the title of "Grand Master of the Flowers."

Misho originated from the *Saga* School, whose purpose it was, from the beginning, to depict the natural beauty of living plants and scenes within the confines of a flower receptacle.

It is related that one day the Emperor Saga went out in a boat to the "Island of the Chrysanthemums" in a pond near the Imperial Palace. Here he broke off some sprays of chrysanthemums, which he took back to the palace and placed in a vase, without altering the stems or leaves in any manner. Upon perceiving the beauty of the flowers in the vase, the Emperor is said to have admonished his attendants that if they ever put flowers into a vase they should imitate his method.

KADO AND SOKA

In connection with *Misho-ryu* flower arrangement, the words *Kado* and *Soka* have special significance. *Soka* means the art, using technical skills, of arranging plant materials as they grow naturally. *Kado* (or the Way of Flowers) means to attain, through the arranging of flowers, cultivation of mind, purity of heart and body, and contentment in one's daily life. Spiritual and material life are united in *Kado*, and the flower arrangement created by a thoughtful man will reflect his spiritual depth.

SANSAI RULE

The *Misho* method of flower arranging is based upon the *Sansai* rule, a spiritually symbolic theory holding that Heaven (male) is round, and Earth (female) is square, so that all things are born of the two combined. Were they separate and apart, nothing would be brought into existence.

In *Fig. 17*, illustrating the *Sansai* rule, Heaven, Man and Earth are located at points 1, 2 and 3, respectively, of the corners of the square. No line of the design (in the Formal type) extends beyond the limits of an erect triangular one-half of the square.

An arrangement to the left of the vertical axis commonly called a "right-hand" arrangement, is designated *Master Style*, while that to the right of the axis, commonly referred to as a "left-hand" arrangement, is designated *Guest Style*.

FUNDAMENTAL FORMS OF MISHO-RYU CLASSICAL ARRANGEMENT

Done in strict conformity with the *Sansai* rule there are three

Fig. 16

Fig. 16, Shoka: Informal with Nejime.

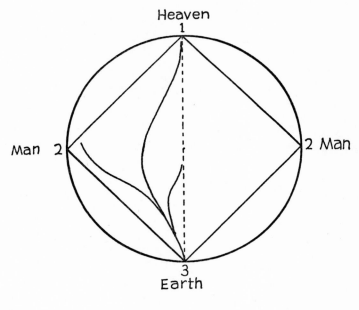

Fig. 17

Fig. 17, Sansai Rule (Misho-ryu).

basic forms of the *Misho-Ryu* method: Formal (*Shin*), Semi-formal (*Gyo*), and Informal (*So*).

Flexibility is allowed in measurements of the main lines, the types of plant material employed being the controlling factor. The main stem (Heaven) may be as much as three times the height of the container without violating the basic rules.

The *Misho-Ryu* teaches two forms of *Ikenobo:* the standing form and the sidelong form. The standing form is used when the arrangement is to be placed *on* something, while the sidelong form is used in a hanging container. The sidelong form is also employed as the top-most arrangement in a container which has two or more openings.

Stems or branches must always be odd in number. The Semi-formal arrangement is considered more graceful, due to its greater spread. Added width is effected by a deeper bend in the Heaven line.

In the Informal *Misho-Ikenobo,* the Heaven line is still more curved and the arrangement spreads more than the Semi-formal, which results in a more elegant appearance.

Variations may be accomplished by having either an individual main branch, or the supports to any main branch, placed in a more flowing position.

MISHO ARRANGEMENTS IN LOW BOWLS

There is an informal *Misho-Ryu* arrangement designated as *Lateral Design* which bears a rather close resemblance to the *Moribana Waterviewing* form, though the composition is of the *Ikenobo* tradition. It is illustrated by *Fig. 18.*

Where a round bowl is used, as shown in *Fig. 19,* the flowers are arranged in the center of the container, and the height of the Heaven (*Shin*) placement is 2½ times the diameter of the bowl.

In a rectangular or oval bowl, flowers are not placed in the center. One grouping may be erect, the other (made with the same material) slanting sideways. The Heaven line in the erect grouping is 1½ times the diagonal of the bowl; the length of the Heaven line in the sidelong grouping is determined by how much visual weight is needed at that point to balance the visual weight of the erect grouping. The use of two groupings lends variety and interest and, as well, establishes proportion between the plant material and the container. *(Fig. 20).*

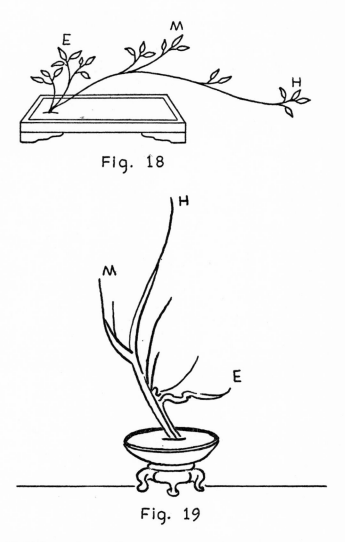

Fig. 18

Fig. 19

Fig. 18, Misho-ryu Lateral Design. Fig. 19, Misho-ryu Ikenobo in round bowl.

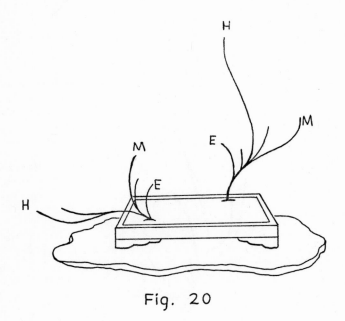

Fig. 20

Fig. 20, Double Misho-ryu-Ikenobo.

When branches, flowers, roots, etc. have been divided into two or more groupings within a low bowl, these groupings should, when viewed together, comply with the *Sansai* rule.

HANGING BOAT ARRANGEMENT

In the Hanging Boat arrangement, the Heaven line is regarded as a sail; the Earth line represents an oar, rudder or anchor. *(Fig. 21).*

SIDELONG FORMS (INFORMAL)

In *Misho-Ryu,* the unalterable rule for placing two arrangements in one bamboo tube or vase *(Fig. 22)* is that the flowers be arranged in slanting (or sidelong) position in the upper part, and in erect (or standing) position in the lower. (Note the difference between this double arrangement and that of the *Shoka* method as shown in *Fig. 16).*

In the double-root arrangement for hanging, the arrangement in the lower part of the container is allowed to slant sideways or stand erect, and the arrangement in the upper part slants in the opposite direction and hangs down parallel to the container. *(Fig. 23).*

SHO-FU-RYU METHOD

The present head of the *Sho-fu-ryu* is Mrs. Josui Oshikawa, well known in many sections of the United States as a lecturer and teacher. The school was founded by Mrs. Oshikawa's uncle, a military man and scholar, skilled in the art of *Ikebana,* about the beginning of the Twentieth Century and at a time when persons other than the Japanese people, living in Japan, or natives of Japan who had come to live in Western-style homes, began to wonder how they could arrange flowers to suitably decorate their new-style homes.

"Foreigners" began settling in Japan when the founder was still young. He recognized that something other than the classical forms of flower arrangement was needed. He also realized that the old flower forms could be fittingly modified to meet the needs of the settlers. Upon this premise, he began creating less conventional forms of arrangement, which are still in vogue in Japan and in this country.

In creating *Ikenobo* arrangements, the founder of *Sho-fu-ryu* retained the basic groups of Heaven, Man and Earth, but added two

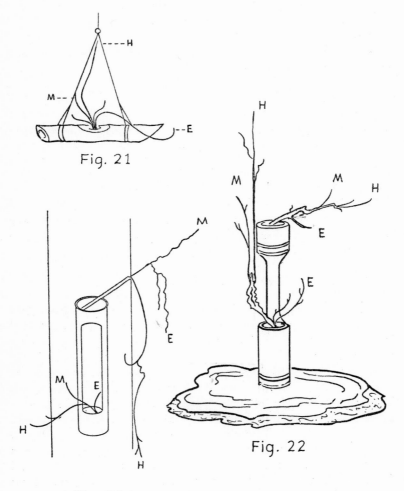

Fig. 21

Fig. 22

Fig. 23

Misho-ryu-Ikenobo Forms: Fig. 21, Hanging Boat Arrangement. Fig. 22, Two
arrangements in bamboo vase. Fig. 23, Double-root arrangement for hanging.

devices called *Mikoshi* and *Tome* to broaden the arrangement and make it more becoming to the western style architecture.

The *Sho-fu-ryu* uses the popular *Shin, Soe* and *Tai* designations in *Ikenobo, Moribana* and *Nageire* forms, but for the sake of consistency, the main placements will continue to be referred to herein as Heaven, Man and Earth.

The supporting branches to the main placements in the *Ikenobo* forms are called:

Soe-Ushiro—In back of Man.
Shin-Ushiro—In back of Heaven.
Tai-Ushiro—In back of Earth.
Shin-Mae—In front of Heaven.
Maezoe—In front of Man.

Any long-stemmed flower, grass or tree branch is suitable for the *Ikenobo* arrangement. Containers are of the traditional type; branches are held in place by a *kubari,* with a *komi* as a stay, as in other methods of the classical *Ikenobo.*

Figures 24-32 give a fair picture of several forms of arrangement which might well be modified to complement the décor of the modern American home.

SIMPLE IKENOBO

The measurements of the main lines in a *Sho-fu-ryu Ikenobo* arrangement (Fig. 24) are variable, according to the type of materials used, but the rules for the *Simple Ikenobo* are an excellent guide. The measurements are:

Heaven (*Shin*)	—Curved branch 2½ times the height of the container, added to its depth. Flowers, if any on the branches, face to the front.
Back of Heaven (*Shin-Ushiro*)	—Less length than main Heaven branch; designates North and should be kept sparse.
Front of Heaven (*Shin-Mae*)	—Less length than back attribute, and has more body than Back of Heaven.
Man (*Soe*)	—2/3 length of Heaven, with tip pointing in opposite direction to that taken by Heaven and Earth groupings.
Back of Man (*Ushiro-Zoe*) and	—Placed between the Heaven and Man main branches, with tips turning upwards.

Front of Man (*Maezoe*)	
Earth (*Tai*)	—1/3 length of Heaven. Flowers or leaves, if any on branch, face Heaven group. Earth branch points toward shoulder of arranger, with tip turned upward toward Heaven.
(*Tai-Shin*) and Valley (*Tani*)	—Placed between the Heaven and Earth main branches, with Valley shorter than Earth or Tai-Shin.

IKENOBO WITH NEJIME

In an Informal or Semi-Formal *Ikenobo* arrangement, a group of flowers, numbering from three large blossoms to as many as nine or more small ones, called *nejime,* may be used as a substitute for the Earth group. The *nejime* is not used if there are flowers in the Heaven and Man groups. The tallest flower in the *nejime* should measure about 1/3 the height of the main Heaven line, *(Fig. 25).*

DOUBLE IKENOBO ARRANGEMENT

A bamboo tube with two openings is used for this arrangement. The upper arrangement is made of tree or shrub branches, the lower one of flowers, *or,* two or more species of flowers may be used. Instructions for creating this arrangement are:

Upper Arrangement (Form A or Form B)

Heaven and Man	
(*Shin*)	(*Soe*) exchange positions.
Heaven (*Shin*)	—Length equal to height of container.
Man (*Soe*)	—2/3 length of Heaven, shaped and placed just like *Heaven* line in *Simple Ikenobo.*
Earth (*Tai*)	—1/3 length of Heaven.

Lower Arrangement (Form A), Fig. 26.

Heaven (*Shin*)	—Extends to top of container.
Man (*Soe*)	—2/3 length of Heaven; keep sparse.
Earth (*Tai*)	—1/3 of Heaven.

If the upper arrangement is right-handed, then the lower one must be left-handed, and vice-versa, so that the Man branch in the upper section of the vase will appear to be an extension of the Heaven branch in the lower section.

Lower Arrangement (Form B) Fig. 27.

Heaven —Tip just inside opening and directly beneath *nemoto*
(*Shin*) of upper arrangement.

Man —2/3 the length of Heaven.
(*Soe*)

Earth —1/3 the length of Heaven. Keep sparse.
(*Tai*)

SIMPLE SINGLE IKENOBO IN BAMBOO VASE, Fig. 28.

Heaven —1½ times height plus depth of container; otherwise,
(*Shin*) follow measurements for *Simple Ikenobo,* keeping arrangement sparse.

Earth —Extends forward; approximately ½ of opening should
(*Tai*) be free of flowers.

STANDING BOAT ARRANGEMENT, Fig. 29.

Heaven —About length of boat, using plant material of erect
(*Shin*) growth. Otherwise, follow measurements for *Simple Ikenobo.*

HANGING ARRANGEMENT IN CRESCENT MOON

Follow rules of *Simple Ikenobo.* Keep Heaven within crescent. May be right-hand or left-hand design. Use vines or other trailing materials. *(Fig. 30).*

SUNABACHI ARRANGEMENT

This is an *Ikenobo* arrangement in a low bronze bowl. It is very attractive done with strong, wide leaves, combined with berries, fruits or flowers (very little of the latter, as the large leaves are the featured element). Branches may likewise be used, if preferred. The rules for the *Simple Ikenobo* are followed in this form of arrangement. *(Fig. 31).*

HANGING FLOWER ARRANGEMENT

This arrangement is done in accordance with the rules for the *Simple Ikenobo,* but trailing plant material must be used. The arrangement should hang so that the *nemoto* will be at eye level of a standing person. *(Fig. 32).*

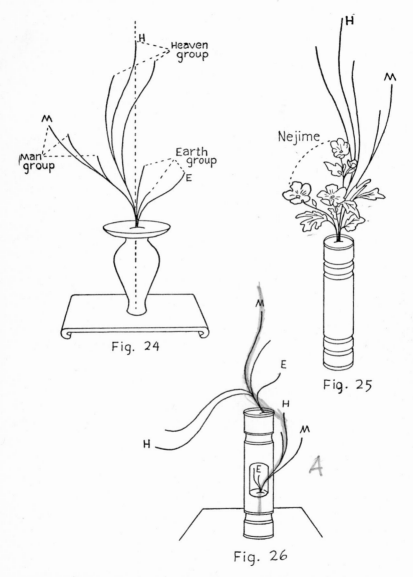

Fig. 24

Fig. 25

Fig. 26

Sho-fu-ryu-Ikenobo Forms: Fig. 24, Semi-formal. Fig. 25, with Nejime. Fig. 26, Double arrangement, Form "A."

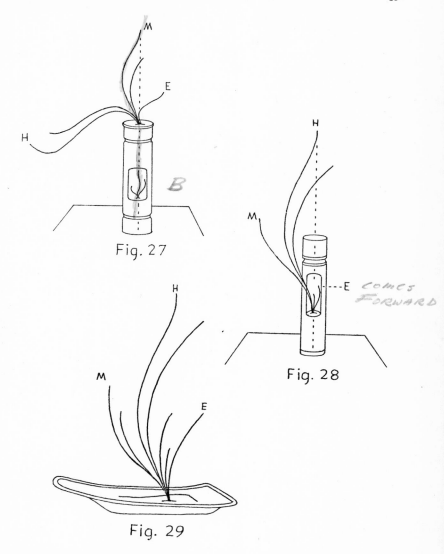

Fig. 27

Fig. 28

Fig. 29

Sho-fu-ryu-Ikenobo Forms: Fig. 27, Double arrangement, Form "B.' Fig. 28, Single Ikenobo in bamboo vase. Fig. 29, Standing Boat arrangement.

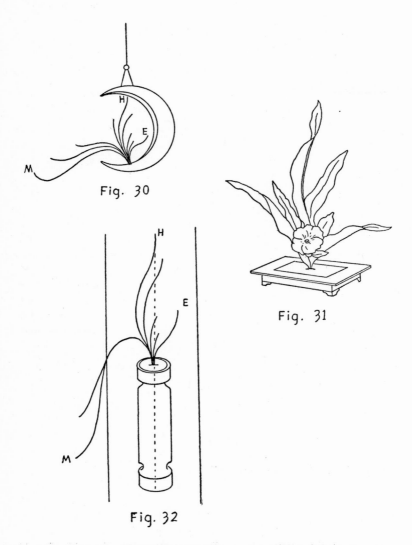

Fig. 30

Fig. 31

Fig. 32

Sho-fu-ryu-Ikenobo Forms: Fig. 30, Hanging arrangement in Crescent Moon. Fig. 31, Sunabachi arrangement. Fig. 32, Hanging arrangement.

CHAPTER 3

NAGEIRE ARRANGEMENTS

IKENOBO-NAGEIRE

First, let it be understood that *Nageire* is *not* a separate and distinct "school" but a naturalistic method of *Ikenobo*. The form is a scalene triangle (no two sides the same). The three main lines generally meet at either the left-front or right-front corner of the vase, with the lines usually inclining forward toward one shoulder of the arranger, their tips forming a triangle.

Modern Nageire tends to express individuality. There are no rigid rules for the interrelationship of Heaven, Man and Earth.

Tall vases are used, and there is practically unlimited latitude in the choice of materials, vases and controls.

Nageire arrangements of the *Ikenobo* School may be done in three forms, with variations of each. Figures 33-41, inclusive, illustrate the positions of the main lines in three variants each of the three basic forms in present-day *Nageire*, in which the Heaven line may take diverse angles and directions. The positions of Man and Earth are determined by how Heaven is placed.

UPRIGHT FORM Figs. 33-35.

Heaven (*Shin*)	—1½ times the height plus width of container, measured from its rim. Main Heaven line inclines slightly forward.
Man (*Soe*)	—¾ the length of Heaven.
Earth (*Tai*)	—½ the length of Heaven.

INCLINING FORM Figs. 36-38.

Heaven (*Shin*)	—1½ times the height plus width of container, measured from its rim. Heaven line inclines forward and appears more horizontal than vertical.

Man   —¾ the length of Heaven.
(*Soe*)
Earth   —½ the length of Heaven.
(*Tai*)
HANGING FORM Figs. 39-41.
Heaven   —Inclines forward in hanging position; may hang below
(*Shin*)   base on which container rests.
Man   —¾ the length of Heaven.
(*Soe*)
Earth   —½ the length of Heaven.
(*Tai*)

SHO-FU-RYU-NAGEIRE

The *Nageire* arrangement is considered by many teachers as the form most easily mastered by Westerners.

The literal translation of *Nageire* is "thrown in." This does not mean that *Nageire* is less an art than *Ikenobo* or *Moribana,* but that it reflects a naturalness achieved through carefully considered freedom from complexity.

Nageire resembles *Ikenobo* in that it retains the three groups of Heaven (*Shin*), Man (*Soe*) and Earth (*Tai*). As in *Ikenobo,* it is a triangular form of arrangement, with each grouping likewise triangular in itself.

Discrimination in combining plant material is important, for the finished arrangement should appear as a group of amicable growing plants.

Any and all kinds of branches (bare, with leaves or flowers, or bearing fruits or berries), flowers and grasses are suitable, so long as the rule is observed that they be harmonious.

SEASONS EXPRESSED BY DENSITY OF ARRANGEMENT

The Japanese calendar year is divided into "The Four Seasons," and all activities revolve around the seasons. Flower arrangement is no exception, the density of the arrangement being governed by the season, as:

Spring   —Moderately full, expressing growth (different stages of development if only one species of flower used.)
Summer —Full; an abundance of flowers.

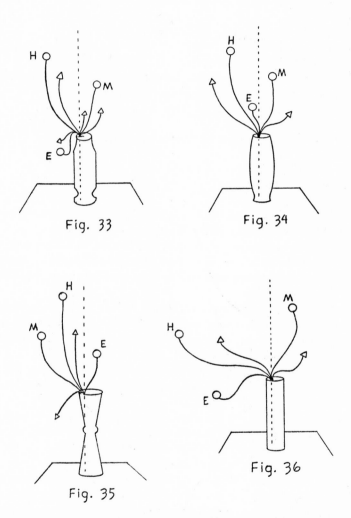

Ikenobo-Nageire: Fig. 33, Basic Upright Form. Figs. 34 and 35, Variation of Upright. Fig. 36, Basic Inclining Form.

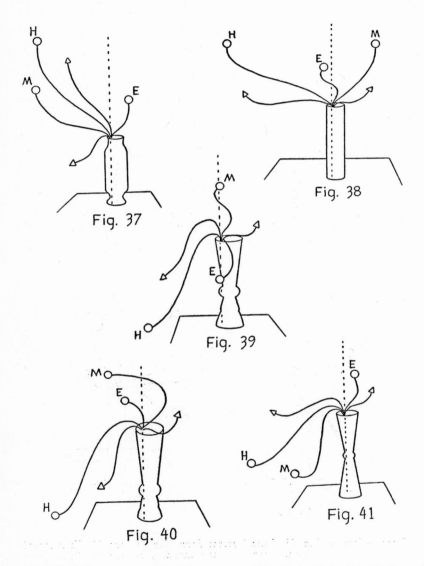

Ikenobo-Nageire: Figs. 37 and 38, Variations of Inclining Form. Fig. 39, Basic Hanging Form. Figs. 40 and 41, Variations of Hanging Form.

Fall —Moderately full, employing flowers that are less than perfect; dry and/or broken branches; dry seed-pods.

Winter —Sparse; evergreen tree branches most popular choice.

A few of the forms of *Sho-fu-ryu-Nageire* which appear to be adaptable to modern living are:

SINGLE FLOWER ARRANGEMENT

This is a form associated with the Tea Ceremony. Single-flower arrangements can be most charming, and answer a definite need when flowers are scarce. The camellia is particularly desirable for this arrangement.

There is genuine grace in the single-flower arrangement (Fig. 42), due to its simplicity. Care must be exercised to keep the tip of the main branch over the point where it emerges from the container, and the flower used should be fresh and crisp. A round flower is more appropriate than one of irregular shape in the one-flower arrangement.

It is a rare thing for a Japanese flower arrangement to be done with just one flower, the exceptions being the Tea Ceremony form and the Fall arrangement, when a single flower would symbolize the coming of Winter.

STANDING FORM, FIG. 43.

Heaven —Equal to height, plus greatest width, of vase, measured
(*Shin*) from rim. Place upright, just left of center of vase. Add attributes to main Heaven line as needed.

Man —2/3 height of Heaven. Use same materials as for
(*Soe*) Heaven, *or* bud if flowers only are in arrangement. Man branch points to left shoulder.

Body —No set height; not always needed. If Heaven and Earth
(*Do*) are of tree branches, Body should be of flowers; if flowers only are used, body should be of dark-colored or fully opened blossoms.

Valley —Shortest part of arrangement. Use twigs from shrub,
(*Tani*) or dark or fully-opened flower.

Earth —½ of Heaven; tip points to right shoulder. Additional
(*Tai*) branches or flowers may be added only *behind* Earth branch. Earth may be of same material as other two main groupings, *or* of same material as Body and **Valley**.

Fig. 42

Fig. 42, Single Flower Arrangement (Sho-fu-ryu).

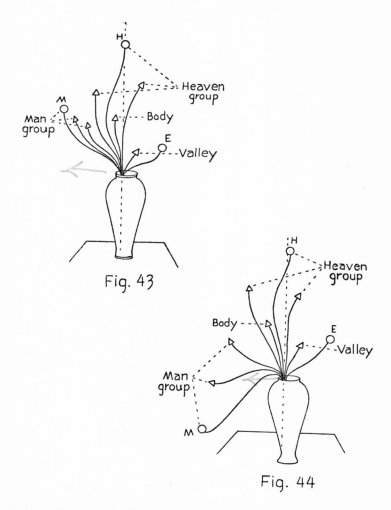

Sho-fu-ryu-Nageire: Fig. 43, Basic Standing Form. Fig. 44, Basic Flowing Form.

FLOWING FORM, FIG. 44.

The *Flowing Form* of the *Sho-fu-ryu-Nageire* arrangement is variously called by other teachers "Slanting" or "Inclining" form.

Use vines or flexible materials, or interesting branches combined with lively-colored flowers. Obey the laws of natural growth. A tree branch for Earth would be inappropriate if flowers are used for Heaven and Man. If the Heaven and Man branches are devoid of flowers, then the Earth and Valley placements may be of flowers, in which case the Earth group is called *nejime*. If Heaven and Man are of flowering branches, then the *nejime* may be of flowers of contrasting form and color.

In the *Flowing Nageire*, Man is the longest branch, though not the tallest, as is shown by the following directions:

Man
(*Soe*)
—Equal to height of vase, plus its greatest width, measured from rim. Man main branch points toward left shoulder. This should be a long, trailing branch. Add additional branches as needed, maintaining a triangular shape in the Man grouping, with tips of branches pointing upward.

Heaven
(*Shin*)
—Equal to 1½ times the height of the vase. Made of same material as Man. Shaped like Heaven branch of Ikenobo. Place in upright position a bit to left of center of vase. Tip must be over base. If a single branch appears weak, add additional branches as needed.

Body
(*Do*)
—No definite height; sometimes not needed. Used to add density to arrangement, and is placed between Heaven and Man. Use branch or open flower.

Valley
(*Tani*)
—No definite height, but shortest part of arrangement. Dark or open flower most effective.

Earth
(*Tai*)
—½ the height of Heaven, tip pointing to right shoulder. Use either same material as for Heaven and Man, *or* same material as for Body and Valley. If needed, branches or flowers may be added only *behind* Earth branch.

SOGETSU-NAGEIRE

The *Sogetsu-ryu*, founded by Sofu Teshigahara in 1926, teaches two methods of flower arrangement: *Nageire* and *Moribana*. The principal placements in both methods have the same names and standard measurements.

"HEAVEN, MAN, EARTH"

Regardless of the literal translations of *Shin*, *Soe* and *Hikae*, in order to maintain consistency in identifying the three main lines of an arrangement, we shall call these placements "Heaven," "Man," and "Earth" as we have done in our discussion of other methods. The supplemental placements (*jushi*) will be referred to as "fillers."

We have, then, as the three main lines:

Heaven   —The longest line and first main branch or stem.
(*Shin*)

Man   —Second main branch or stem and medium length line.
(*Soe*)

Earth   —The third main branch or stem, and shortest line.
(*Hikae*)

In addition to these main lines, we have:

Fillers   —Subordinate or additional supplements, which may be
(*jushi*)   used freely. They must be shorter and of different
           lengths than the main lines which they support. They
           act not only as supports to the main lines, but as fillers
           to widen the arrangement.

The standard measurements of the main lines differ according to size of arrangements:

LARGE ARRANGEMENT

Heaven   —2 times depth plus height of container
(*Shin*)

Man   —¾ of Heaven
(*Soe*)

Earth   —½ of Man
(*Hikae*)

STANDARD ARRANGEMENT

Heaven   —1½ times depth plus height of container
(*Shin*)

Man   —¾ of Heaven
(*Soe*)

Earth   —¾ of Man
(*Hikae*)

SMALL ARRANGEMENT

Heaven   Depth plus height of container
(Shin)
Man   —¾ of Heaven
(Soe)
Earth   —¾ of Man
(Hikae)

HOW TO USE FLOWERS

The longest and strongest line (Heaven or *Shin*) faces the viewer and turns up to the sun. If flowers are used, the largest and best are used for Heaven; otherwise, the best flower is for Earth (*Hikae*). Usually the Heaven and Man placements are greens or branches, while Earth (*Hikae*) is of flowers. The back of the arrangement is considered North and farthest from the sun; place poor material and buds in rear.

BASIC FORMS OF SOGETSU-RYU

The two basic forms for both *Moribana* and *Nageire* arrangements are:

1) The basic upright form (where Heaven (*Shin*), the longest line, is upright.)

2) The basic slanting form (where Heaven (*Shin*), the longest line, is tilted).

In giving directions for each form, the standard length measurements for the three main lines will be used, with the reminder, however, that measurements vary in large and small arrangements.

Basic Upright Nageire (Standard lengths), Fig. 45.

Heaven   —1½ times height plus width of vase; slant slightly
(Shin)   forward.
Man   —¾ of Heaven; split end of branch and fasten to Heaven
(Soe)   branch, tilting toward left shoulder.
Earth   —¾ of Man; slant toward right shoulder.
(Hikae)
Fillers —One in front and another in back of Earth.
(Jushi)

Do not allow material to rest on lip of container.

Basic Slanting Nageire (Standard lengths), Fig. 46.

Heaven   —1½ times height plus width of vase; tilt diagonally
(Shin)   toward left shoulder.

Man —¾ of Heaven; place in back of Heaven at a 15 deg. tilt.
(*Soe*)

Earth —¾ of Man; tilt diagonally toward right shoulder.
(*Hikae*)

Fillers —One in front and another in back of Man. Add addi-
(*Jushi*) tional fillers as desired.

ABBREVIATION OF MAIN BRANCH NAGEIRE, FIG. 47.

This arrangement is made of two placements: Heaven (*Shin*)
and Earth (*Hikae*), with Man (*Soe*) omitted. Have triangle in
Heaven and fillers, and in Man and fillers, as usual. Materials are
placed in any corner of the vase, but all material leans away from
the vase. Heaven leans diagonally to right front. Earth tilts diagonally forward to left. Measure Heaven and Earth branches the
same as if Man were present in the arrangement.

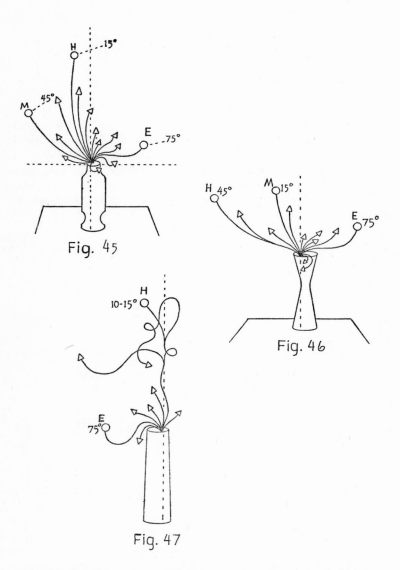

Fig. 45

Fig. 46

Fig. 47

Sogetsu-Nageire: Fig. 45, Basic Upright Form. Fig. 46, Basic Slanting Form. Fig. 47, Abbreviation of Main Branch Arrangement.

CHAPTER 4

HEIKA ARRANGEMENTS

The characteristic love of plants and trees by the Japanese people of ancient times has resulted in the art of flower arrangement as it presently exists. *Ikebana* owes its origin to this characteristic, arising from the nature of the Japanese people.

With few exceptions, *Heika* arrangements are done in tall vases, baskets or bamboo tubes. Generally, an ornamental base is placed under the arrangement. Where the height of the vase is about equal to its diameter, then a short legged stand (*kwadai*) or the tall slender stand is used to supply the height necessary for good proportion between the vase and the materials used in it. Special techniques with Heika arrangements are shown on pages 21-23, 28.

MISHO-RYU HEIKA

The *Misho-ryu* stresses *elegance* as a prerequisite to acceptable *Heika* arrangements. Elegance is an intangible and variable quality, which may be attained in many ways—through intricacy, simplicity, magnificence, tidiness, ornateness, vigor or repose. However expressed, *Heika* arrangements are without purpose if elegance is lacking.

In contrast to *Moribana* arrangements where plant materials are closely massed in a low flat bowl, *Heika* arrangements present a more informal and less complicated form. Flowers and plants are arranged according to their inherent character.

(*Note:* We will find in our discussion of the *Non-Realistic Forms* of the *Ohara-ryu* that a different conception of *Moribana* and *Heika* is projected.)

Generally, the height of the Heaven (*Tai*) placement is 1½ times the height of the vase, but this measurement can be increased or decreased according to the material used. Other measurements are

left to the discretion of the arranger, though the general form of a
scalene triangle is maintained.

Man is *Soe,* and Earth is *Tome.* The earth grouping spreads out a
great deal to give a look of naturalness, and as a consequence, the
Earth main line is not so clearly defined as is usual. Filler materials
in this form are also called *Tome.* To simplify the instructions that
follow, the word *Tome* is used for either the Earth line or the Earth
grouping.

The basic forms of *Misho-ryu Heika* are:

UPRIGHT FORM, FIG. 48.

Heaven (*Tai*)	—Upright branch placed just to left of center.
Supplement to Heaven (*Tai-No-Soe*)	—Insert shorter branch of same material as Heaven, just back of Heaven branch.
Earth (*Tome*)	—Insert 3 stalks of grass (or other "loose" material), maintaining different lengths, to left of Heaven.

Insert close to rear center of grouping, 2 stalks of grass (or other
"loose" material). This grouping is shorter than Heaven but taller
than the Earth grouping, and not only unites the Heaven and Earth
groups but also serves to cover the stems at the front of the arrangement.

SLANTING FORM, FIG. 49.

Heaven (*Tai*)	—Insert strong, forceful branch or rugged dead branch just left of center, and tilt toward left shoulder.
Man (*Yu*)	—Insert curved branch close to Heaven line, and slant to point just above left shoulder.

Insert at same point as Heaven branch, 2 young green sprouts,
arranging them to appear as if they were growing out of the Heaven
branch near the top.

Earth (*Tome*)	—Insert 3 flowers of different lengths in front and to left of Heaven, letting longest extend forward toward right to complete triangular form established by three main branches.

SIDEWAY FORM, FIG. 50.

Heaven (*Tai*)	—Place branch just to left of center, allowing it to extend forward and upward. This takes

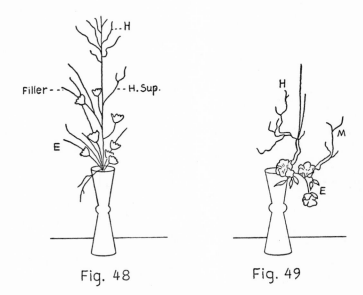

Fig. 48

Fig. 49

Misho-ryu-Heika: Fig. 48, Basic Upright Form. Fig. 49, Basic Slanting Form.

a slant, but it must not touch the lip nor hang below the rim of the container.

| Front Supplement to Heaven (*Tai-no-mae-zoe*) | —About ½ the length of Heaven, emerging from same point as Heaven, but taking more frontal direction. |

Insert a short grouping in front of Heaven main lines, and tilt slightly forward.

| Earth (*Tome*) | —Group five composite flowers with short stems of different lengths, and insert near center of vase. This grouping leaves container at center front. |

CLIFF FORM, FIG. 51.

Heaven (*Tai*)	—Insert rugged and irregularly shaped branch to left of center of opening, and tilt it over rim of container at left front corner.
Man (*Yu*)	—Insert at point of Heaven placement and just back of Heaven branch, a short branch in upright position.
Earth (*Tome*)	—Insert a grouping of short-stemmed flowers of different lengths just in front of Heaven group, allowing it to face right shoulder.

HANGING FORM, FIG. 52.

Heaven (*Tai*)	—Use vine with curled-back tip, hanging down from opening of vase at a point about half way between center and left front corner of bamboo vase.
Man (*Yu*)	—Relatively short branch with piece of heavy fruit or large flower on end, leaving mouth of container just left of center.
Earth (*Tome*)	—A very short grouping of flowers with own foliage in erect position between Heaven and Man, extending only slightly forward between these two main placements, and crossing rim of container between center and left front corner.

OHARA-RYU HEIKA

The *Ohara-ryu* designates the three principal placements in both the *Heika* and *Moribana* arrangements as *Subject Stem* (Heaven),

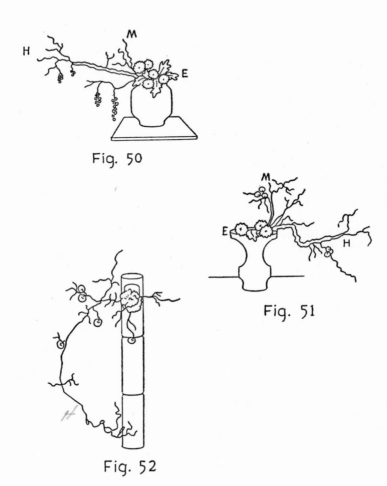

Fig. 50

Fig. 51

Fig. 52

Misho-ryu-Heika: Fig. 50, Basic Sideway Form. Fig. 51, Basic Cliff Form.
Fig. 52, Hanging Form.

Secondary Stem (Man) and *Object Stem* (Earth.) The fillers are *Intermediaries.*

For *Heika*, the vase or jar is used. Less floral material is required than for *Moribana* arrangements. Only one-fourth of the mouth of the vase is used; the remaining three-fourths should be free of flowers.

If the *natural* lines and curves of an interesting or broken branch cross an erect placement, it is *not* considered a fault.

Standard measurements of the main lines are:

Heaven *(Subject Stem)* —At least 1½ times the height of the vase, measured from the rim; line extends forward toward left shoulder.

Man *(Secondary Stem)* —2/3 the length of Heaven; placed upright, meeting Heaven line at mouth of vase.

Earth *(Object Stem)* —½ length of Heaven; place at other side of Heaven from Man line, extending forward toward right shoulder.

The basic forms of *Heika* are *Upright, Slanting* and *Cascade.*

UPRIGHT FORM (BASIC), FIG. 53.

Heaven *(Subject Stem)* —Upright.

Man *(Secondary Stem)* —Tilting forward toward left shoulder.

Earth *(Object Stem)* —Pointing toward right shoulder.

Figures 54-56 show examples of variations of the Upright Form, from which it will be noted that Heaven is always the most erect line in the arrangement.

SLANTING FORM (BASIC), FIG. 57.

Heaven *(Subject Stem)* —Tilting toward left shoulder.

Man *(Secondary Stem)* —Upright in background.

Earth *(Object Stem)* —Placed on other side of Heaven, and slanting toward right shoulder.

VARIATION OF SLANTING FORM (FIG. 58)

Here the Heaven line is still the longest, but not the most upright main branch.

CASCADE FORM (BASIC), FIG. 59.

Heaven	—Trails in a cascade to near, or below, bottom
(*Subject Stem*)	of vase, at left front.
Man	—Erect, and in back of Heaven.
(*Secondary Stem*)	
Earth	—Upright, slanting toward right front.
(*Object Stem*)	

VARIATION OF CASCADE FORM

The difference between this variation and the basic Cascade Form lies in the changed positions of the Man and Earth placements. *(Fig. 60)*

All of the above described forms are capable of infinite variations, depending upon the shape of the vase and the types of plant material selected to go into them.

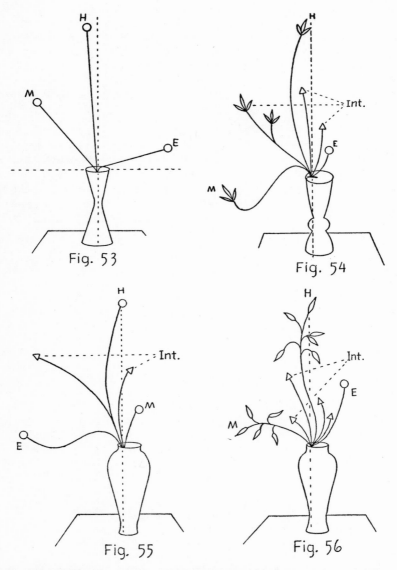

Ohara-ryu-Heika: Fig. 53, Basic Upright Form. Figs. 54, 55 and 56, Variations of Upright.

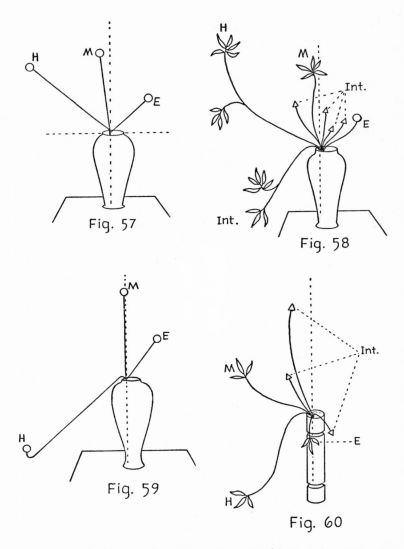

Ohara-ryu-Heika: Fig. 57, Basic Slanting Form. Fig. 58, Variation of Slanting. Fig. 59, Basic Cascade Form. Fig. 60, Variation of Cascade.

CHAPTER 5

MORIBANA ARRANGEMENTS

The Ohara-ryu was founded by Unshin Ohara, about 1890. Until that time, he was known best as a master of classical flower arrangement. With the introduction into Japan of many colorful and exotic Western plants, the founder Ohara was inspired to arrange these flowers. Because of their short stems, however, they were unsuitable for the classic forms, so Unshin Ohara began creating original designs, the result being the birth of the popular *Moribana* arrangement, an informal treatment of plant life.

Unshin Ohara died in 1916, and his son Koun Ohara succeeded him as Master of the Ohara School. This second-generation Master trained special teachers of the *Moribana* and *Heika,* among them his son Houn Ohara who, at the death of his father in 1938, became the third-generation Master of the *Ohara-ryu.*

MORIBANA OF THE OHARA-RYU

Before his death Koun Ohara divided *Moribana* into two general classes:
1) The *Moribana* emphasizing color.
2) The *Moribana* emphasizing natural beauty.

According to the *Moribana* stressing color, flowers are arranged in a low bowl, with careful attention to colors and forms. Some of the techniques of grooming plant materials to achieve this objective are shown on pages 23-24.

The *Moribana* stressing natural beauty depicts the infinite beauty of nature within a small bowl, emphasizing the natural growth of the plant materials used.

Figure 61 indicates four points within a bowl, any one of which is appropriate for flowers. The one point chosen will determine the form or pattern of the design to be made.

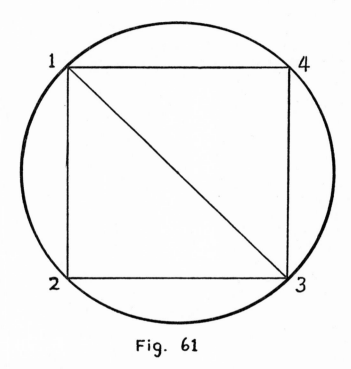

Fig. 61

Fig. 61, Possible locations of arrangement in bowl (Ohara-ryu-Moribana).

If Point 1 has been chosen, then the flowers will be arranged within the triangle formed by Points 1, 2 and 3. This does not mean that the plant material must occupy the *whole* space, but that it must be contained within such space. Scalene triangles, typical of all Japanese flower arrangement, may be defined within the area bounded by the three points mentioned, to allow for variations in the flower form.

The *Moribana* arrangement is much fuller than any classical form. The union of stems and the flower holders are concealed by low, bunched masses of cypress, lycopodium, or the like. Club moss, native to Japan, is unavailable to us, and our Western moss is unsuitable because it would soil the water. Any feathery green plant which has lasting qualities and which will not deteriorate in water may be substituted for the club moss.

The standard measurements of the main lines in Ohara-ryu *Realistic Moribana* arrangements are:

Heaven   —Width of bowl, plus its depth.
(*Subject Stem*)
Man   —2/3 the height of Heaven.
(*Secondary Stem*)
Earth   —1/2 the height of Heaven.
(*Object Stem*)

Intermediaries are added to fill in unpleasing open spaces between the main lines and to unify the three principal parts of the composition. Intermediaries may be of the same material as Heaven, Man or Earth, but they must always vary in length. Unlike the classical forms, some intermediaries may be placed lower than the main Man and Earth lines if by so doing the design is made to look more natural.

BASIC FORMS OF OHARA-RYU MORIBANA

There are four basic forms of the Moribana which we should learn to construct before we try to "branch out" into free style arranging. They are:

UPRIGHT FORM, FIG. 62.

Heaven   —Width of bowl, plus its depth; placed in
(*Subject Stem*)   back corner, in erect position.
Man   —2/3 of Heaven; placed at left front of bowl
(*Secondary Stem*)   and tilted toward ~~right~~ *left* shoulder.

Earth   —½ of Heaven; placed at ~~left~~ *right* front of bowl
(*Object Stem*)   and tilted toward ~~left~~ *right* shoulder.
(Both Man and Earth extend forward).

SLANTING FORM

Heaven and Man exchange positions; otherwise, this form is fundamentally the same as the Upright Form. *(Fig. 63)*

CASCADE FORM

The Cascade Form is similar to the Slanting Form. Trailing plant material is used. The rule being that no part of Heaven may touch the base (or floor), this arrangement must be placed on a shelf, mantel, bookcase, tall stand, etc. *(Fig. 64)*

WATER-REFLECTING FORM

A wide expanse of water must be left visible. This is made possible by use of sparse amount of plant materials and by placing the main branches close together and very near outer edge of the bowl. *(Fig. 65)*

All lines in a *Moribana* arrangement are curved, in one degree or another, and all are of unequal lengths. Rhythm of movement is thus obtained.

The whole theory of *Moribana* is to express a purpose, and to that end all elements incorporated into the arrangement should be selected with infinite care and discrimination, keeping in mind the purpose intended to be expressed.

SHO-FU-RYU MORIBANA

There are six groups in any *Sho-fu-ryu Moribana* arrangement, each of which may consist of any number of branches or flowers. These groups are:

Heaven (*Shin*), which includes *Mikoshi*
Man (*Soe*)
Earth (*Tai*)
Valley (*Tani*)
Filler (*Tome*), gives illusion of boundary between Earth and sky.
Body (*Do*)—density

Composite diagrams showing the placement of the holders in the bowl, the placement of stems in the holders, and the direction taken by each main placement for each of the various forms of *Sho-fu-ryu*

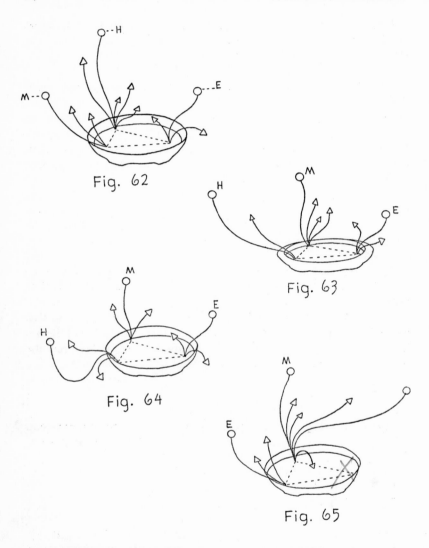

Fig. 62

Fig. 63

Fig. 64

Fig. 65

Ohara-ryu-Moribana; Fig. 62, Basic Upright Form. Fig. 63, Basic Slanting Form. Fig. 64, Basic Cascade Form. Fig. 65, Water Reflecting Form.

Moribana are included for guidance. If you will study *Figs. 66-73,* inclusive, with the instructions below, and take the instructions step by step, you cannot fail to make good Moribana arrangements.

SIMPLE MORIBANA, FIGS. 66-67.

Heaven —1½ to 2 times the greatest dimension of the bowl.
(*Shin*)   Insert in holder between lines 6 and 7 (tip over base). Add supplements in front and back of Heaven, as needed.

Man —2/3 the height of Heaven. Place in holder on Line 6,
(*Soe*)   with tip over Line 5. Add supplements in front and back of Man, as needed.

Body —No set height; not always needed; used to add density
(*Do*)   to arrangement, Place in holder in front of Heaven and to right of Man groups, on and above Line 6.

Earth —1/3 the length of Heaven. Place in holder on Line 4
(*Tai*)   and extend forward between Lines 3 and 4. Add supplements if needed, between Earth main branch and Heaven group.

Valley —No set height. Place between Heaven and Earth groups.
(*Tani*)   Valley conceals stem ends and holders and is usually needed. Use wide-open or dark colored flowers for Valley.

Filler —½ the length of Heaven. Place in holder between Lines
(*Tome*)   7 and 8, tip over base. Add needed supplements in front of this branch. Keep sparse.

DIVIDED ROOT MORIBANA

Principal Group (Keep confined within space defined by Lines 4 and 7)

Heaven —1½ to 2 times greatest dimension of bowl.
(*Shin*)

Man —2/3 height of Heaven.
(*Soe*)

Earth —1/3 length of Heaven.
(*Tai*)

Filler —½ the height of Heaven.
(*Tome*)

Subordinate Group (Keep confined within space defined by Lines 2 and 3). Figs. 68, 69.

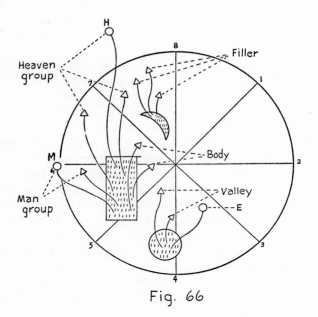

Fig. 66

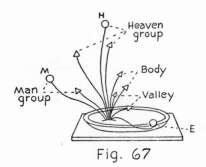

Fig. 67

Sho-fu-ryu-Moribana Basic Form: Fig. 66, Locations of holders and plant
materials in bowl. Fig. 67, Front view.

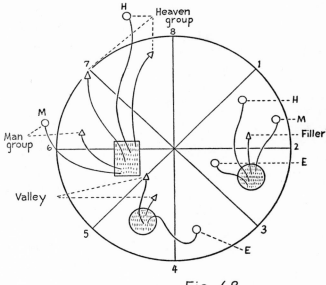

Fig. 68

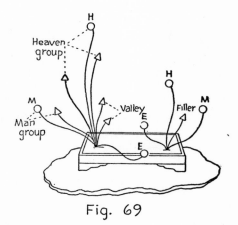

Fig. 69

Sho-fu-ryu-Moribana Divided-root Form: Fig. 68, Locations of holders and plant materials in bowl. Fig. 69, Front view.

Heaven —3/5 length of Heaven in Principal Group.
(*Shin*)

Man —2/3 length of Heaven in Subordinate Group.
(*Soe*)

Earth —1/3 length of Heaven in Subordinate Group.
(*Tai*)

Filler —½ length of Heaven in Subordinate Group.
(*Tome*)

WATER-VIEWING MORIBANA

Use plant material which grows upright by nature, preferably reeds and other plants indigenous to water. There is no restriction as to numbers of kinds, in either flowers or branches. This arrangement may be made with only one kind of plant. The surface of the water is an integral and important part of the desired effect, so no less than one-half its surface is left exposed, Figs. 70, 71.

Man —Length of diagonal of bowl. Place in holder below
(*Soê*) Line 2 so that tip of branch points toward Line 5; let tip turn upward.

Heaven —1½ to 2 times width of bowl. Place upright above
(*Shin*) Line 2, tip over base. Use same material as for Man.

Body —No set height; not always needed, but if used it must
(*Do*) be placed between Heaven and Man, just above line 2.

Earth —1/3 height of Heaven. Place near Line 3, with tip point-
(*Tai*) ing toward Line 4. Use different material than in Heaven and Man.

Valley —No set height. Place behind main Earth branch, and
(*Tani*) keep lower than any other part of arrangement. Use material that grows close to ground.

Filler —½ the height of Heaven. Place behind and to right
(*Tome*) of Heaven, just below Line 1.

DIVIDED WATER-VIEWING MORIBANA

(with Principal arrangement to Right Front)

Principal Group (Keep this grouping confined to area between Lines 1 and 3)

Heaven —1½ to 2 times width of bowl. Place above Line 2, tip
(*Shin*) over base. Add supplements in front and in back of Heaven, if needed.

Man —2/3 of Heaven. Place in front and to left of Heaven,

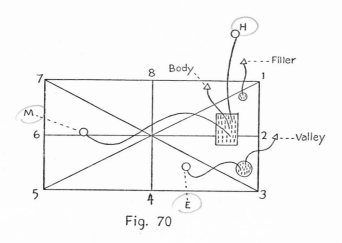

Fig. 70

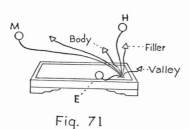

Fig. 71

Sho-fu-ryu-Moribana Water-viewing Form: Fig. 70, Locations of holders and plant materials in bowl. Fig. 71, Front view.

MAN

(Soe)	below Line 2. Supplements may be added in front and in back of Man, if needed.
Body *(Do)*	—Not always needed. If used, place between Heaven and Man, below Line 2.
Earth *(Tai)*	—1/3 length of Heaven. Place on Line 3, or a little above it, between Man branch and corner of bowl. Add supplements as needed. Keep shape triangular.
Valley *(Tani)*	—No set length. Place behind and to right of Earth, just above Line 3. Keep very low.
Filler *(Tome)*	—½ length of Heaven. Place behind and to right of Heaven. Add supplements as needed, but keep grouping sparse.

Subordinate Group

Simple Heaven-Man-Earth arrangement on Line 7, in rear corner of bowl.

Earth points toward Earth of Principal Group.

Heaven is about 3/5 the length of Heaven in Principal Group.

(Fig. 72)

WATER-VIEWING MORIBANA

Divided Arrangement with Principal Arrangement to Right Rear

Principal Group

Heaven *(Shin)*	—1½ to 2 times width of bowl. Place upright, tip over base, between Lines 1 and 2. Add supplements in front and back of Heaven main branch, if needed.
Man *(Soe)*	—2/3 length of Heaven. Place in front and to left of Heaven below Line 2. Add supplements in front and in back of Man main branch, if needed.
Earth *(Tai)*	—1/3 of Heaven. Place in front and to right of Heaven near Line 3. Add supplements as needed between Earth and Heaven groups.
Valley *(Tani)*	—No set length. Place behind and to right of Earth at about Line 2. (Lowest part of whole Principal Group).
Filler *(Tome)*	—½ length of Heaven. Place behind and to right of Heaven near Line 1. Add supplements in front if needed, but keep growth sparse.

Subordinate Group

Small "Heaven-Man-Earth" arrangement on Line 5, with Heaven

equal to 3/5 of Heaven in Principal Group. Earth branch points toward Earth of Principal Group. *(Fig. 73)*

All of the forms described and illustrated are susceptible of variations. The divided-root arrangement may have the Principal Group at left front or right front, or at left rear or right rear.

IKENOBO-MORIBANA

The Moribana arrangement as taught by the present-day *Ikenobo* schools is similar to *Nageire* in that it is fundamentally triangular and its main branches are *Shin*, *Soe* and *Tai* (Heaven, Man and Earth).

A low, flat container (*suiban*) is used, and the width of the bowl is the standard in measuring the length of the main branches. If the container is round, its diameter is taken as the standard; if it is rectangular, oval or triangular, the longest side is the standard.

Use of only two or three varieties of flowers will insure greater unity and will better express the mood or environment constituting the dominant theme.

Standard measurements of the main lines are:

Heaven —1½ times diameter or length of bowl, plus its height.
(*Shin*)

Man   —¾ the length of Heaven.
(*Soe*)

Earth   —½ the length of Heaven.
(*Tai*)

The arrangement is made at a point in the right or left front corner of a rectangular bowl, and at a point 1/3 the length of an oval or oblong bowl.

Three important considerations in the *Moribana* form are *height*, *width* and *depth*, and these conditions should be expressed by the Heaven, Man and Earth placements. The longest line (Heaven) is not necessarily the highest in the arrangement, nor is Earth, the shortest placement, always the lowest.

The popular pin-point holder, called *kenzan*, is used to hold the design in place.

The three basic forms of Ikenobo-Moribana are: *Upright Form*, *Inclining Form*, and *Hanging Form*.

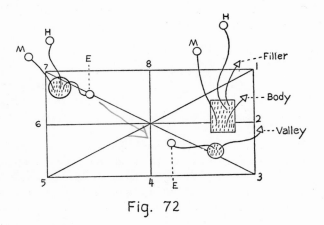

Fig. 72

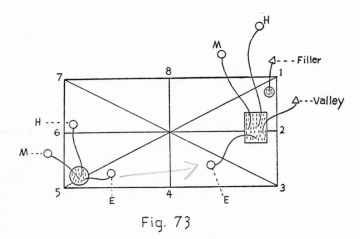

Fig. 73

Sho-fu-ryu-Moribana Water-viewing Form: Fig. 72, Principal arrangement to front. Fig. 73, Principal arrangement to rear.

Since the *Ohara-ryu* is the source for all *Moribana* forms regardless of the variants or methods taught by other schools, the illustrations of the *Ikenobo-Moribana* basic forms will help you create those arrangements without detailed instructions. *(Figs. 74-82.)*

Bear in mind always that even though you may add as many supplements as you desire, you must not abuse the privilege, for Japanese flower arrangements are delicate and lovely things, *featuring three main lines; and this linear pattern should be so well planned as to be perceptible at first glance.*

MISHO-RYU MORIBANA

The *Misho-ryu* classifies *Moribana* arrangements as 1) Natural and 2) Colorful. The Natural arrangement portrays a scene from nature in a single bowl. The Colorful arrangement stresses color effects.

According to this method, the *Moribana* is composed of five elements, whose standard measurements are:

1) Heaven   —1½ times the diameter of the bowl.
   (*Tai*)
2) Man   —2/3 the height of Heaven.
   (*Yu*)
3) Earth   —½ the height of Heaven *or* 1/3 that of Man.
   (*So*)
4) Earth Attributes—No rule for height so long as they are not
   (*Right So* and   of same height.
   Left So)
5) Relative   —Three low flowers between Heaven and
   (*Tsunagi*)   Man.

Unless otherwise indicated, these basic measurements apply to all of the forms hereinafter described.

RIGHT FORM ARRANGEMENT

(Arranged in right half of bowl, Fig. 83)

1) Heaven   —Insert in right rear ¼ of bowl, with tip
   (*Tai*)   pointing to right shoulder.
2) Man   —Insert in right front ¼ of bowl and bend
   (*Yu*)   forward toward left shoulder.

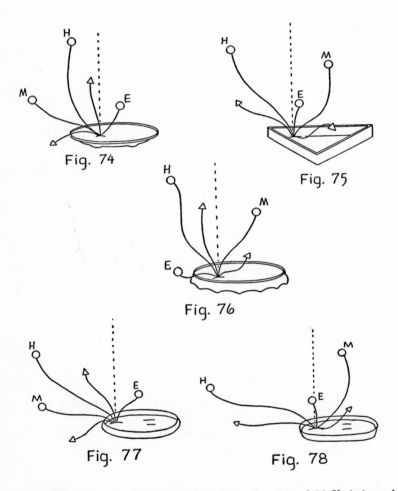

Ikenobo-Moribana: Fig. 74, Basic Upright Form. Figs. 75 and 76, Variations of Upright. Fig. 77, Basic Inclining Form. Fig. 78, Variation of Inclining.

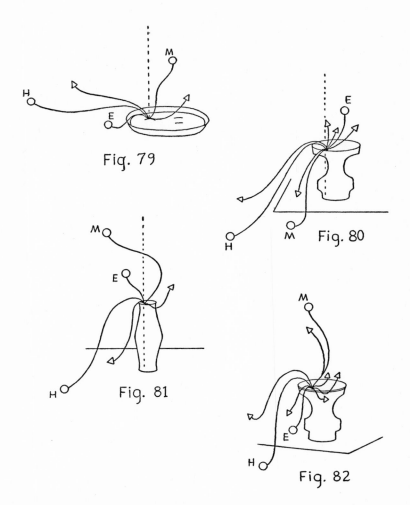

Fig. 79

Fig. 80

Fig. 81

Fig. 82

Ikenobo-Moribana: Fig. 79, Variation of Inclining Form. Fig. 80, Basic Hanging Form. Figs. 81 and 82, Variations of Hanging Form.

3) Earth   —Place in erect position to left of Heaven,
   (*So*)   in right back ¼ of bowl.

4) Relative   —No fixed height; insert in space between
   (*Tsunagi*)   Heaven and Man.

5) Earth Attributes —Add at about half-way position near right
   (*Right So* and   edge of bowl.
   Left So)

6) Supplement to —Insert in back ¼, slightly in front of Earth.
   Man   Point in same direction as Man.
   (*Yu
   Supplement*)

7) *Uzumi*   —Insert bunched cypress or the like, kept
                    low to cover holder, in right front corner of
                    bowl.

LEFT FORM ARRANGEMENT

Arranged in left half of rectangular or oval bowl (Fig. 84).

1) Heaven   —Insert in rear left corner, and point toward
   (*Tai*)   left shoulder.

2) Man   —Insert in left front corner and point toward
   (*Yu*)   right shoulder.

3) Earth   —Insert just to right of Heaven; point toward
   (*So*)   right shoulder.

4) Right Earth   —Insert a little to right and in rear of Earth.
   Attribute   Keep low.
   (*Right So*)

5) Left Earth   —A little shorter than Right So, and placed just
   Attribute   in rear and to left of Earth.
   (*Left So*)

6) Relative   —Insert different material from Heaven, Man or
   (*Tsunagi*)   Earth, in front of Heaven and Earth group-
                    ings, and tilt forward.

7) Heaven   —A piece of same material as Relative; insert
   Supplement   in front and to right of Heaven, and extend
   (*Tai-no-soe*)   forward.

8) Earth   —Insert in front and a little to right of Earth,
   Supplement   and tilt toward right just above surface of
   (*So-no-soe*)   water.

Cover *kenzans* with bunched cypress or its equivalent.

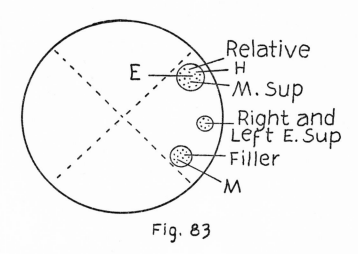

Fig. 83

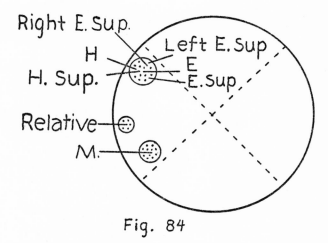

Fig. 84

Misho-ryu-Moribana: Fig. 83, Right Form Arrangement. Fig. 84, Left Form Arrangement.

FRONT FORM ARRANGEMENT

(Arranged in front portion of bowl. Represents a shore line with body of water beyond. Keep flowers low so water will be visible. Fig. 85.)

1) Heaven (*Tai*) —Insert in right front ¼ of bowl and tilt toward right shoulder. No set measurement for this line.

2) Man (*Yu*) —Insert toward front and to left of Heaven grouping, and tilt toward left shoulder.

3) Earth (*So*) —Insert erect placement to left and back of Heaven.

4) Relative (*Tsunagi*) —Insert toward front, to left of Heaven, keeping stem short.

5) Left Earth Attribute (*Left So*) —Insert short bunched cypress or the like at left and to rear of Earth.

6) Right Earth Attribute (*Right So*) —Same material as *Left So*; insert just to right of Earth; little shorter than *Left So*.

7) Supplement to Heaven (*Tai-no-soe*) —Insert in front and to right of Earth; longer than usual.

8) Supplement to Man (*Yu-no-soe*) —Insert short bunches of cypress or its equivalent to right and rear of Man.

9) *Uzumi* —Insert short cypress (or equivalent) to conceal holder.

REAR FORM ARRANGEMENT

(Occupies back portion of bowl. Represents opposite shore of a large body of water. Fill bowl to brim with water, Fig. 86.)

1) Heaven (*Tai*) —No fixed height; insert to right of center, in back of bowl, and tilt toward right front.

2) Man (*Yu*) —Insert at extreme left rear.

3) *Earth* (*So*) —Insert twig of young erect growth between and to left of Heaven and *Right So*.

4) Heaven —Insert small twigs of same material as Heaven

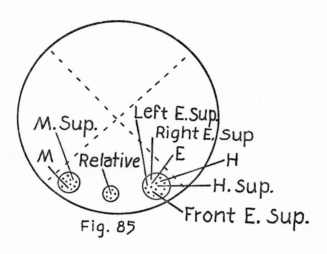

Fig. 85

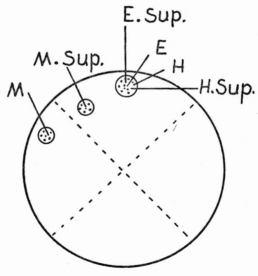

Fig. 86

Misho-ryu-Moribana: Fig. 85, Front Form Arrangement. Fig. 86, **Rear Form** Arrangement.

	Supplement (*Tai-no-soe*)	branch, a little in front of Heaven.
5)	Right Earth Attribute (*Right So*)	—Insert twig of different type shrub, to right of Earth. Keep low.
6)	Supplement to Man (*Yu-no-soe*)	—A few flowers may be added when space indicates they are needed, and short sprigs of cypress, lycopodium or the like, added to conceal holders.

STANDING FORM ARRANGEMENT

(Occupies left end of bowl. Erect form of arrangement, employing three kinds of flowers, Fig. 87).

1)	Heaven (*Tai*)	—Insert one flower (as iris) with 3 leaves, adding 2 leaves in rear to complete group, in left rear ¼ of bowl.
2)	Earth (*So*)	—One flower and 3 leaves in front of Heaven.
3)	Heaven Supplement (*Tai-no-soe*)	—One flower and 3 leaves inserted to right of Earth.
4)	Man (*Yu*)	—Insert a few round flowers with own foliage (no two same height) in most frontal position.
5)	Left Earth Attribute (*Left So*)	—Insert 3 leaves of iris, if iris used, just behind *Right So.*
6)	Right Earth Attribute (*Right So*)	—Insert asparagus fern, or its equivalent, in front and to right of *Left So.*
7)	Supplement to Heaven (*Tai-no- Tome*)	—Same material as for *Right So*, placed to left front of Heaven.
8)	Relative (*Tsunagi*)	—Chrysanthemums or other small round flowers, grouped and inserted in front and to right of Heaven Supplement.
9)	Add 2 more iris leaves (if iris used) inserting them to right of Heaven Supplement.	

THE NATURAL ARRANGEMENT
(Occupies left end of oblong bowl. Scenic—Using plants that grow at water's edge, with those of mountains or fields, Fig. 88).

1) Heaven (*Tai*) —Insert tall, erect tree branch (height to be determined proportionately to bowl) in left rear ¼ of bowl.

2) Earth (*So*) —Insert shrub branches or large leaf to left and rear of Heaven.
Insert short pieces of same material as Heaven grouping, in front ¼ of bowl.

3) Heaven Supplement (*Tai-soe*) —Insert to right of earth, and tilt to extend over surface of water.
Insert flower of some sort, with hanging head, in front of Earth, and tilt toward right front of bowl.

(*Note:* Because the above described arrangement is *scenic* only, Man (Yu) is omitted.)

DECORATIVE FORM
(For home decoration; no restriction as to measurements, choice of materials, choice of colors, or selection of container)

Heaven (*Tai*) —Use large flower with healthy leaves, and insert in right end of container, tilting flower head diagonally forward toward left shoulder.

Man (*Yu*) —Use a large flower that has chromatic strength of color, and insert to left and front of Heaven.

Earth (*Tome*) —Use large, serrated or irregularly formed leaf, and insert to left and a little in rear of Heaven.
Add additional foliage low, between Heaven and Man, to fill out form of arrangement.

(Above is just one example of a Decorative Form; there are many others.)

SEASONAL ARRANGEMENTS
Many dates are observed in Japan through the medium of flower arrangements—created with flowers, shrubs, vegetables, tree branches, grasses, etc. all fresh at the time of the celebration.

There are also arrangements depicting a pond; mountains and valleys; woodland scenes; swamps and marshes; seaside views; the Four Seasons etc.

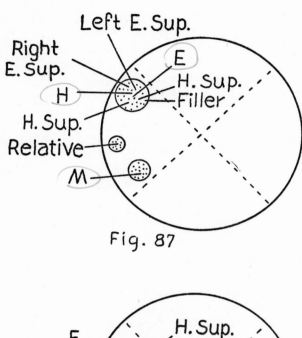

Fig. 87

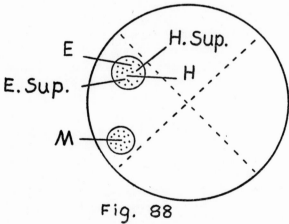

Fig. 88

Misho-ryu-Moribana: **Fig. 87**, Standing Form Arrangement; **Fig. 88**, Natural Arrangement.

Seasonal arrangements are made along the same lines as those described in detail above. They may be in any form, so long as the requirement is observed that the plant material used be in season.

A strong branch devoid of foliage, or even a dead branch, symbolizes the bleakness of Winter. Materials which appear serene and peaceful are suggestive of Autumn. Summer arrangements are profuse, and Spring arrangements are loose and spreading.

SOGETSU-RYU MORIBANA

The *Sogetsu-ryu* is today one of the outstanding modern schools of flower arrangement in Japan. The founder's innate artistic temperament precluded his acceptance of the old *Ikebana* traditions and methods, and he determined to work out a method of his own, unlike that of any other teacher. Teshigahara felt that the teachers of *Ikebana* who worked within prescribed rules were mere craftsmen. In training his students he urges that they look ever forward, creating new, fresh and animated styles.

Although Teshigahara himself is a creative modern artist, his methods still show trends of the past.

As mentioned in our discussion of the *Sogetsu-Nageire* forms, the three main lines in the Moribana are Heaven (*Shin*), Man (*Soe*), and Earth (*Hikae*), with the supplements and fillers designated *Jushi*.

Standard measurements for both *Moribana* and *Nageire* arrangements of the *Sogetsu-ryu* are given in the chapter titled "*Nageire*." Keep in mind that the measurements for standard, small and large arrangements, vary.

PLACEMENT OF KENZANS

The *kenzan* (pin-point holder) is used for *Moribana* arrangements. It may be placed at any corner (or corners) of an imaginary square located in the center of the bowl, as illustrated in *Fig. 89*. If the arrangement is to be right-hand, the *kenzan* is placed to the left. If the arrangement is to be left-hand, the *kenzan* is placed to the right. It is never placed in the center of the bowl for any of the basic forms.

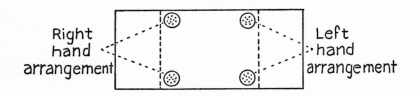

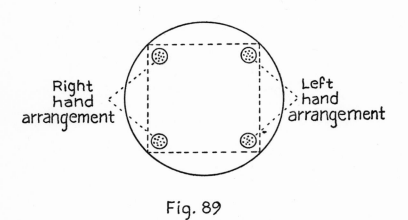

Fig. 89

Fig. 89, Location of holders in bowl (Sogetsu-ryu-Moribana).

The direction taken by the Earth (*Hikae*) line determines whether the arrangement is right or left-hand.

MEASUREMENTS OF SLANTS BY DEGREES

Because it is impossible to transfer to paper in true perspective the slant taken by various lines in the composition, the tilt will be determined by the number of degrees a line is removed from the central axis of a half-circle. The circumference of a full circle is, of course, 360 degrees, but you will usually be working within 180 degrees. Figure 90 illustrates the placements by degrees of the three principal lines in the basic *Sogetsu Upright Form*.

BASIC UPRIGHT MORIBANA (Fig. 91)

(Standard Lengths)

Heaven —1½ times the diagonal plus the height of the bowl.
(*Shin*) Anchor Heaven branch or stem in back center of holder; tilt 10-15 deg. diagonally to left front. If there are leaves and/or flowers on the Heaven branch, their faces should be turned toward the arranger.

Man —¾ of Heaven; place in left front of holder and tilt
(*Soe*) diagonally toward left front at about 40-45 deg.

Earth —¾ of Man; place in right front of holder; tilt 75
(*Hikae*) deg. diagonally toward right front, and have the face up so that it looks toward Heaven.

Fillers —One in front of Heaven, between Heaven and Man,
(*Jushi*) and two between Heaven and Earth. Additional fillers may be added as desired. Keep fillers within three points of a triangle.

BASIC SLANTING MORIBANA (Fig. 92)

Heaven —1½ times diagonal plus height of bowl. Place holder
(*Shin*) to back, either corner. Heaven hangs over water. Exchange Heaven and Man. If Heaven in right corner, tilt diagonally toward left front at about 40-50 deg.

Man —¾ of Heaven; place in center rear of holder; slant in
(*Soe*) same direction as Heaven but at about 15 deg.

Earth —¾ of Man; place in right front part of holder, slanting
(*Hikae*) at about 75 deg. diagonally toward right front (in left-hand design).

Fillers —Two filler stems are inserted between Heaven and
(*Jushi*) Man; another in front, and one at side of Earth. Add

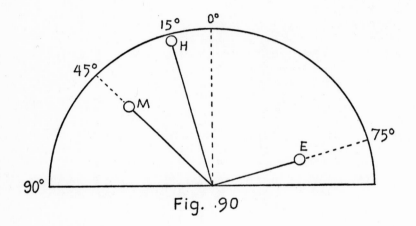

Fig. 90, Slants by degrees (Sogetsu-ryu arrangements).

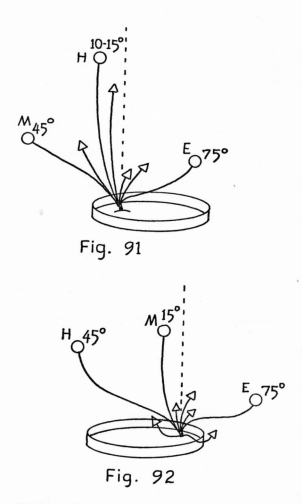

Fig. 91

Fig. 92

Sogetsu-ryu-Moribana: Fig. 91, Basic Upright Form. Fig. 92, Basic Slanting Form.

fillers as desired. Cover holder with plant material but don't let it lie under water.

OPEN VARIATION MORIBANA

Upright Form (Fig. 93)

Increase space between Heaven (*Shin*) and Man (*Soe*) to give open look. Holder in a front corner of bowl. Heaven leans 10-15 deg. diagonally away from Man and toward rear instead of forward. Use fillers sparingly to maintain open effect.

MAIN BRANCH INTERCHANGE MORIBANA (Fig. 94)

Heaven (*Shin*)	—In same position as in basic form; tilt at about 15 deg. diagonally toward front.
Man (*Soe*)	—Tilt at 75 deg. diagonally forward toward front corner of bowl.
Earth (*Hikae*)	—Tilt at 45 deg. diagonally forward in opposite direction from Man line.

In the *Main Branch Interchange Moribana,* as well as *Nageire,* the positions of Man and Earth are reversed.

DIVIDED FORM MORIBANA ARRANGEMENT (Fig. 95)

Place Heaven (*Shin*) and Man (*Soe*) in one holder, and Earth (*Hikae*) in the other. The holders are placed one to front, one to back, diagonally opposite each other. They should be at two points of an imaginary square inside the bowl, as shown in Figure 89. Use standard measurement for Earth line in the small arrangement, and always arrange in a large bowl to accent the surface of the water and emphasize the width of the arrangement. *(Figure 95)*

ALL-AROUND VIEW HORIZONTAL MORIBANA

Heaven (*Shin*)	—Tilt at 85-90 deg. toward left front.
Man (*Soe*)	—Tilt at 60-70 deg. to right front.
Earth (*Hikae*)	—Slants straight back at 75 deg.
Fillers (*Jushi*)	—Keep short. This arrangement is very low in the center, and is suitable for a dining table.

(Figure 96)

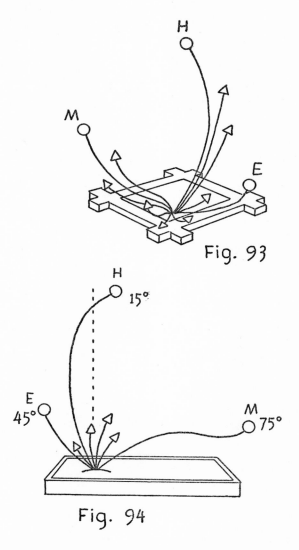

H

Fig. 93

H
15°

E
45°

M
75°

Fig. 94

Sogetsu-ryu-Moribana: Fig. 93, Open Variation Form. Fig. 94, Main Branch
Interchange.

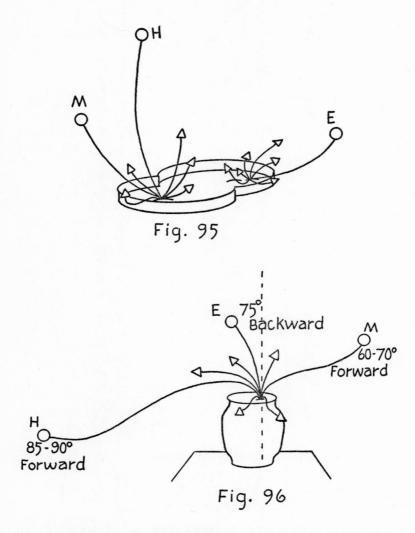

Fig. 95

Fig. 96

Sogetsu-ryu-Moribana: Fig. 95, Divided Form. Fig. 96, All-around View Horizontal Form.

CHAPTER 6

THE MORIMONO ARRANGEMENT

A *Morimono* arrangement is a still-life composition, consisting of a grouping of plant materials, fruits, vegetables, or other products of nature such as branches, stones, things from the sea, and figures of animal life, in which the dominant theme is interpreted more by the combination of the elements used than by the choice and dominance of plant materials. The elements may be combined in any way desired. Where fruits or vegetables are included, they must be fresh, in season, and of attractive form and color.

Morimono arrangements are made in platters, bowls, shallow dishes, on large leaves (such as banana or palm), bamboo rafts, small boards, trays, or on anything that is not decorated.

MORIMONO OF THE MISHO RYU

The *Misho-ryu* teaches three kinds of *Morimono:* (1) The *Vegetable Morimono*, using products of especial natural beauty and color, such as eggplant, mushroom, bamboo sprout, melons of various kinds, cucumber, turnip, radish, beet root, etc. Vegetable greens with curled edges are attractive in combination with the vegetable forms.

(2) *Fruit Morimono*, arranged in form similar to the Vegetable Morimono. Grapes are always graceful. Any fruit of distinctive form and color may be used, either alone or combined with foliage or a few flowers. The fruit must be the dominant feature, however.

(3) *Hanamori:* This form is similar to the Moribana except that flowers are arranged on a base or tray instead of in a bowl. Any flower suitable for a Japanese flower arrangement is appropriate for the *Hanamori* form of arrangement.

The most important factor in creating *Morimono* arrangements is to select the plant form intended to be featured, and relate all other elements subordinately to it.

Both material and color should be elegant and distinctive in character. The *strongest characteristic* of an element (the fruit, root, bud, leaf, stem or flower) should be *emphasized* in the arrangement.

Morimono arrangements are sometimes complemented by accessories, such as bronze figurines, scrolls, or even diminutive growing plants. Two separate *Morimono* arrangements, treated as a unit, are effective when staged at different levels, as one on a stand and one on a low base.

MORIMONO OF THE SOGETSU-RYU

Morimono arrangements, according to the *Sogetsu* method, may be done in or out of water, depending upon the characteristic requirements of the materials used. The forms follow rather closely those of the Misho-ryu. *Figures 97-99* are examples of *Sogetsu-Morimono* arrangements.

Another form of *Morimono* arrangement is the *Okibana,* composed of branches and flowers arranged on a base, without water.

FLOATING ARRANGEMENT

To make this arrangement, fill a plate with water and lay a long branch diagonally in it, allowing the tip to extend over the edge. Insert two short branches at its base, to create a triangular form in the branches. Float two large composite flowers near the stem of the long branch. *(Fig. 97).*

SPREAD FLOWER ARRANGEMENT

Lay fruit branch directly on table and place three flowers (forming a scalene triangle) on top of the branch. Insert a few small flowering twigs here and there to soften the lines. This is suitable as a table arrangement. It is temporary, and the flowers must be such as will remain fresh out of water. *(Fig. 98).*

PLATTER DESIGN

Any shallow vessel, board, tray or large leaf will serve as container; vegetables, fruit, small branches, flowers and leaves may be combined in any way desired. *(Fig. 99).*

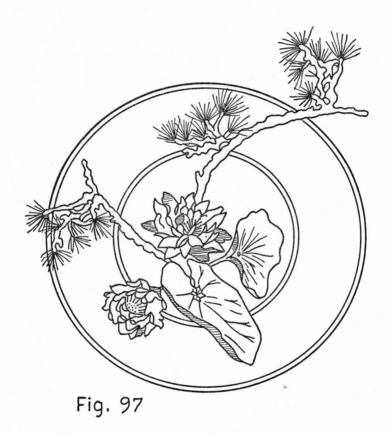

Fig. 97

Fig. 97. Misho-ryu Morimono, Floating Arrangement.
Sogetsu

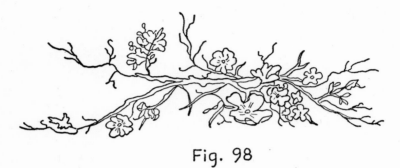

Fig. 98

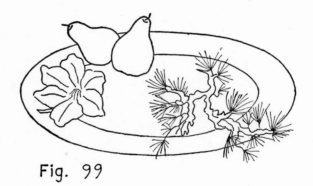

Fig. 99

Sogetsu-ryu-Morimono: Fig. 98, Spread Flower Arrangement. Fig. 99, Platter Design.

CHAPTER 7

MODERN JAPANESE FREE STYLE

OHARA-RYU

While all arrangements of the *Ohara-ryu* up to the past few years depicted nature, the two general classes of arrangement now are differentiated according to their *attitude toward nature* and are called:

1) *REALISTIC (Shajitsu)*, to which grouping belong arrangements stressing natural beauty, as well as those emphasizing color; and,

2) *NON-REALISTIC (Hi-Shajitsu)*, in which natural growth is ignored and materials are considered only for what their color and shape will express symbolically in the hands of a skilled and imaginative arranger.

The Non-Realistic form is, of course, entirely foreign to anything we have ever known about Japanese floral art.

From witnessing the creation by Huon Ohara of a number of Non-Realistic arrangements, I reached the conclusion that this method uses flowers and/or other elements in any way other than what one would normally expect. A large manzanita branch was placed upside down, the smaller branches serving as "legs." With it Mr. Ohara used celosia and a large tight mass of marigolds, several strelitzia and, to give a little airiness, dried fronds of the date palm.

With dried and peeled wisteria tendrils which had been soaked in warm water to make them pliant, he straightened out the branches and shaped them into forms not unlike the strelitzia leaf, using these forms for his linear placements. Then peach gladiola were added, after the tips had been removed and they had been tightly massed to form a single unit.

Flowers are "bunched" to form a mass of color and form, rather than with any idea of showing their individual beauty. This gives a sculptured look to the finished arrangement, and certainly opens a new world to flower arrangers with a bent toward formative art.

Mr. Ohara advises that we master the basic forms first, and then apply them to our own "free styling." In his lectures in the United States, he urged that we be original in our use of plant materials and other products of nature.

Non-Realistic and *Realistic* forms are never combined. You must do either one or the other. For instance, in the manzanita branch arrangement described above, long-stemmed red roses would have been beautiful insofar as color and form are concerned, but they would be entirely inappropriate in a Non-Realistic form of arrangement because they would have to be used in their normal growing position in order that the stems might rest in water.

In the modern *Ohara-ryu,* the basic forms of *Moribana* are classified as:

Upright
Slanting (including Water-Reflecting arrangements)
Cascade
Heavenly
Contrasting

with the Cascade, Heavenly and Contrasting being singled out as more susceptible of variations and free-styling.

In present-day *Ohara Moribana,* the standard measurements are:

UPRIGHT AND SLANTING FORMS

Heaven —Diameter of round bowl, plus its depth.
(*Subject Stem*)
Man —2/3 the height of Heaven.
(*Secondary Stem*)
Earth —2/3 the height of Man.
(*Object Stem*)

HEAVENLY AND CONTRASTING FORMS

The *Heavenly* form is made in a very slender shape, with the main lines of erect-growing plant material. Interrelationship of lengths of the three principal lines is left to the discretion of the arranger. *(Fig. 100)*.

The *Contrasting* form likewise departs from the standard measurements of the earlier Ohara method, and with the freedom allowed in it samplifications, can take the form illustrated by *Figure 101.*

Modern Ohara-Heika is divided into the same general classes as *Modern Ohara-Moribana*. Figures *102 and 103*, respectively, are examples of the *Heavenly Heika* and the *Contrasting Heika* forms.

See pages 23, 25 for Houn Ohara's suggestions for effective grooming of plant materials.

SOGETSU-RYU

Many of the more modern versions of *Moribana, Nageire* and *Morimono* arrangements taught by the *Sogetsu-ryu* are described in the chapters under those titles.

The founder, Teshigahara, is said to be one of the most courageous of the hundreds of Japanese teachers in his departure from restrictive rules. In his classes and in those conducted by teachers who have trained under him, the students are taught basic forms; but when Teshigahara is given free rein, he is likely to create something massive, completely original and bound to capture the attention and respect of all who see it. (Just what Houn Ohara did on his visit to Houston in the Summer of 1958 when he exhibited, in the main lobby of a large bank, a tremendous arrangement expressing his impression of the Texas Gulf Coast country as seen from the air.) It will be interesting to note further accomplishments of these two well-known teachers who are perhaps Japan's foremost exponents of formative art.

One form of modern *Sogetsu* is the *Combination Arrangement (Fig. 104),* done in two containers: a tall vase for the *Nageire,* and a bowl for the *Moribana,* the latter placed in front and toward the side of the taller arrangement. The containers are not required to be of the same color, so long as they harmonize, though the color combination of the entire composition is important. Flavor will be added if the individual arrangements are placed on stands of unequal size and height—the *Nageire* on the taller stand, and the *Moribana* on the lower one.

Now that the scope of Japanese flower arrangement has expanded to include aspects of abstract art, you who will learn the fundamentals of the old *Ikenobo,* as well as the basic and controlling principles of the *Ohara* and *Sogetsu* schools and other modern methods, will be able to give free range to your imagination and

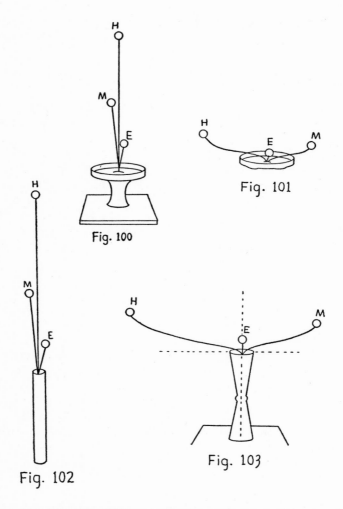

Fig. 101

Fig. 100

Fig. 102

Fig. 103

Modern Ohara-ryu: Fig. 100, Heavenly Moribana. Fig. 101, Contrasting Moribana. Fig. 102, Heavenly Heika. Fig. 103, Contrasting Heika.

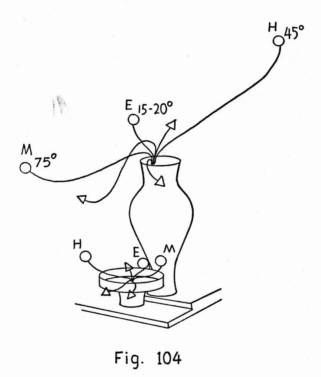

Fig. 104

Modern Sogetsu-ryu: Fig. 104, Combination Arrangement.

impulses in creating flower arrangements "in the Japanese manner," patterned after the forms and methods of whatever *"ryu"* appeals to you.

MISHO-RYU

In addition to the five basic forms of the *Misho-ryu* described in the chapter titled *"Heika"* arrangements, there are the *Combined Form* and the *Mixed Form* associated with this school.

The *Combined Form* is done with materials of drooping character, in hanging containers; the *Mixed Form* may be a combination of *any three* of the five basic forms. These are extremely modern in feeling, and are a departure from the five basic forms.

CHAPTER 8

JUDGING JAPANESE STYLE ARRANGEMENTS

In Japan, flower arrangements are exhibited to be viewed with respect and appreciation. They are *not* judged, but are expected to be interpreted by the observer. True to the American flair for competition, flower show arrangement classes in this country *are* judged, and awards given.

THE STANDARD SYSTEM OF JUDGING

The Standard System of judging is easy to understand. In order to fairly evaluate the exhibits in a class, a scale of points is used as a guide in judging. One hundred per cent, or 100 points, represents perfection of the exhibit *as a whole*. Each quality determined by its relative importance, is allotted a portion of the 100 points. The total number of points allotted to any quality represents perfection *in that quality*. All exhibits in any one class are evaluated by the same scale of points.

A scale of points serves the dual purpose of informing the exhibitor of the conditions he is expected to meet, and of steering the judge to an equitable decision.

With interest in exhibiting flower arrangements "in the Japanese manner" advancing steadily in Standard Flower Shows, and because all other classes (except certain special ones) are competitive, it would seem only fair to the exhibitors that classes of arrangements in the Japanese manner likewise be judged. In some sections of the United States at the present time, these classes are listed as noncompetitive; in other states they are treated as any other class, and each exhibit point-scored.

Lacking any help from the schools of Japan, we must formulate our own scale of points. Such a scale must be broad enough to apply to each method and form of Japanese flower arrangement, because each has individual characteristics.

Design, for instance, must be viewed in the light of the characteristics associated with the particular method and form named in the class. These characteristics will vary according to teacher. If a specific style is not listed in the Flower Show schedule, then the exhibitor should be required to state on his entry card the name of the Japanese school upon which he has based his exhibit, as well as designate the form of his arrangement (that is, whether formal or informal, upright or slanting, etc.)

Experimental judging of flower arrangement classes "in the Japanese manner" by groups of advanced arrangers has proved a real stimulus for further research and practice.

SCALE OF POINTS

The following scale of points, which seems sufficiently flexible to be adapted to any method, has been used with some success:

SUGGESTED SCALE OF POINTS FOR JUDGING ARRANGEMENTS
IN THE JAPANESE MANNER

Design (*according to particular method*)	40
Suitability of container (base and accessory, if used)	20
Symbolism	30
Distinction	10
	100

BASIC DIVISIONS OF JAPANESE FLORAL ART

In the older tradition, Japanese flower arrangements were divided into two basic groups:

1) *Classical:*
   a) *Rikkwa*
   b) *Ikenobo*
2) *Naturalistic:*
   a) *Nageire*
   b) *Moribana*

Mid-twentieth-century flower arrangement in Japan takes on a different aspect. The classical styles are still taught, of course, but the trend is toward free style and formative art. While variations of the classical forms are taught in the modern schools, fundamentally they follow the principles of the old Ikenobo.

The "new look" in Japanese flower arrangement is a natural development, stemming not alone from western influence, but as well from a revolt on the part of some present-day teachers against traditional restrictions.

Classes of flower arrangements "in the Japanese manner" in Standard Flower Shows must be carefully scheduled to meet the capabilities of the exhibitors, and only judges who are thoroughly familiar with the characteristics of the particular methods and forms of arrangement specified should agree to evaluate the exhibits.

STAGING EXHIBITIONS

From the inception of *Shoka* until the evolvement of certain modern forms of *Ikenobo,* the setting for the *Ikenobo* arrangement was the *tokonoma.* The *tokonoma* has lost much of its traditional significance, though it still remains an important feature in many Japanese homes. There is a trend now toward placing flower arrangements in any suitable location in the home, and when so placed, they are described as "decorative."

In flower shows in this country, modern versions of the *Ikenobo* arrangement should be staged well apart and against a plain background, so that each can reflect its own individuality. For the best view, the observer should stand directly in front of and about six feet away from the arrangement, because these designs, as any work of art, are planned to be considered from one vantage position only.

I believe that the *tokonoma* adds charm and authenticity to the show. A simulated *tokonoma* can be constructed for each exhibit. (Having done this on more than one occasion, I can state with authority that it is not too difficult a task. A simple frame of two-by-fours about six feet high, four to five feet wide, and three feet deep, can be lined with corrugated cardboard which can be obtained by the roll from a paper manufacturing house. If several exhibits are to be shown in this manner, the cardboard should not be cut between the exhibits, but just rolled back around the outside of each recessed space, and then brought forward to take care of the next. This plan allows for the hanging of a *kakemono* on the back wall of the *tokonoma,* and makes a very attractive setting for the exhibit.)

BASIC DICTIONARY FOR JAPANESE ARRANGEMENTS

Do Dō	Body (Sho-fu-ryu-Moribana); one or more placements added to give density to the arrangement and unite the main lines.
Enshui-ryu Ehn-shōō'-leh-ōō'	A classical school of Japanese flower arrangement, patterned after the Ikenobo but claiming the Saga School as its origin; distinguished by exaggerated curvature of main lines.
Flower form	Term applied by Japanese to silhouette and pattern of arrangement; does not relate to shape of individual flower.
Form	As used in this text, means type (formal, informal, leaning, standing, etc.) of arrangement.
Gyo Gē-yō'	Semi-formal Shoka and Misho-Ikenobo arrangements; Earth line in Koriu method of Enshui-ryu.
Hana Hä'-nä	Flowers: includes all growing plants, trees and grasses.
Hanamori Hä-nä-mō'-reh	Flowers arranged on a tray or base (a form of Misho-ryu-Moribana).
Heaven-Man-Earth	Even the most casual student of Oriental flower art will recognize this term as identifying the three main placements of floral material. Earth-Air-Water and Father-Mother-Child are less commonly used. To simplify the text, I have used Heaven-Man-Earth throughout when referring to the three basic

lines; however, names adopted by each teacher are mentioned in appropriate places.

Heika
Hāy-ē'-kä

General term for arrangements in vases (Misho-ryu and Ohara-ryu).

Hikae
Hē'-kī

An assistant to *tome* in Misho-ryu-Ikenobo; also the Earth line in Sogetsu-ryu arrangements.

Hi-Shajitsu
Hē-shä-gē'-tsōō

The Non-Realistic method of arranging (Ohara-ryu), in which natural growth is ignored and flowers are considered only for expressiveness of their form and color.

Ike-bana
Ih-keh-bä'-nä

Literal translation: "Living flowers." General term applied to all Japanese flower arrangements.

Ike-no-bo
Ih-kehn'-ō-bō

Literal translation: "Hut by the pond," supposedly referring to the priests' place of retreat in the Temple grounds.

Jushi
Ju'-sē

Supplemental placements to main lines, and/ or fillers, in Sogetsu-ryu Nageire and Moribana forms.

Kado
Kä-dō

"The Way of Flowers"; art of arranging, usually in connection with religious offerings (Misho-ryu). Actually, Kado is a part of the history of Ikebana, and is included in the teachings of Misho-ryu.

Kakemono
Kä-keh-mō'-nō

A scroll placed on the wall of the tokonoma. It usually consists of a painting, a poem, a bit of calligraphy, or a scene of special meaning to the family.

kenzan
khen'-zän

A pin-point holder; used only in low bowls.

komi
kō-meh'

Slender stick placed behind stems to keep materials in place in an erect container where a kubari is used.

Koriu Kō'-leh-ōō'	A method of classical arrangement developed by the Enshui-ryu; resembles the Old Ikenobo more than the Enshui-ryu.
kubari kōō-bä'-rē	Forked stick for holding flowers erect in a narrow-mouthed vase.
kwadai kä-dī'	A short-legged stand used under a flower arrangement.
maezoe mī-eh'-zō-eh'	Supporting branch in front of Man (Sho-fu-ryu).
matagi mä-tä'-gē	Same as kubari.
method	Term used to describe procedure established by founder or teacher of a particular school.
mikoshi mē-kō'-sē	Term applied to one or more placements inserted to one side of main Heaven line and on side opposite to tome (Sho-fu-ryu), which serves to widen the arrangement. (Means "overlook").
Misho-ryu Mē'-shō-leh-ōō'	School of flower arrangement based on Saga teachings and Ikenobo School.
Moribana Mō-rē-bä'-nä	Literal translation: "Piled-up flowers." General term applied to flowers arranged in shallow, flat containers.
Morimono Mō-rē-mō'-nō	General term for fruits, vegetables, flowers or stones arranged for artistic effect according to accepted art principles.
Nageire Nä-gāy-ē'-reh	Literal translation: "Thrown in." A naturalistic form of Ikenobo; general term for arrangements in tall vases or baskets.
nejime nāy-zhe-meh'	Term used by Ikenobo School for shortest group in arrangement when it is made of different materials from other two groups. Nejime takes the place of Earth grouping and

is placed in front of Heaven. (Classical forms).

nemoto
nāy-mō'-tō

The "center of growth"; union of stems above kubari to point of diversion in Ikenobo and Shoka forms.

Object Stem

Designation applied to Earth line by Ohara-ryu.

Ohara-ryu
O-hä'-rä-leh-ōō'

Originator of Moribana arrangement; twentieth-century school of Japanese flower arrangement.

Okibana
O-keh-bä'-nä

An arrangement of branches and flowers on a base, without water (Misho-ryu).

Rikkwa (Rikka)
Rē'-kä

Large, complex form of arrangement; product of early Ikenobo School. Used for Temples and formal Court decorations.

Ryu
leh-ōō'

"School." This term is usually preceded by the name of the founder or teacher of the particular method. (There is no sound for our letter "r" in the Japanese language. This word must be pronounced by "rolling the tongue" over the letters and placing stress on the "oo").

Saga School
Sä'-gä

Supposedly originated during the time of the Emperor Saga (A.D. 810-823). Misho-ryu and Enshui-ryu are both products of the Saga teachings, plus those of the Ikenobo School.

Sansai Rule
Sän'-sī

Symbolic theory holding that Heaven (male) is round and Earth (female) is square, so that all things are born of the two combined. The formal classical Ikenobo of the Misho-ryu follows the Sansai rule.

Secondary Stem

Term used to designate "Man'" line by Ohara-ryu.

Shajitsu
Shä-gē'-tsōō

The Realistic method of arranging flowers (modern Ohara-ryu) in which color and natural beauty are stressed.

Shiki-ita
Sē-kē'-eh-tä

Flat ornamental base placed under a flower arrangement.

Shin
Sēēn

Term applied (by most teachers) to the main branch, commonly called "Heaven," in a Japanese flower arrangement. Term also used to designate Formal Shoka and Formal Misho arrangements.

Shin-mae
Sēēn-mī-eh'

Supporting branch in front of Heaven (Sho-fu-ryu).

Shin-ushiro
Sēēn-ōō-se'rō

Supporting branch in back of Heaven (Sho-fu-ryu).

Sho-fu-ryu
Sō-fōō'-leh-oo'

Twentieth-century school of Japanese flower arrangement.

Shoka (Shokwa)
Shō'-kä

A school of Japanese flower arrangement patterned after the Ikenobo School.

So
Sō

Earth branch in Misho-ryu-Moribana. Informal Shoka-Ikenobo and Informal Misho-Ikenobo forms. Man branch in Enshui-ryu method.

Soe
Sō-eh'

Term applied to secondary branch, commonly called "Man," in most methods of Japanese flower arrangement. Literal translation: "Harmonizer."

Soe-ushiro
Sō-eh'-ōō-sē'-ro

Supporting branch in back of Man (Sho-fu-ryu).

Sogetsu-ryu
Sō-get'-sōō-leh-oo'

School of Japanese flower arrangement founded by Sofu Teshigahara in 1926.

Soka
Sō'-kä

The art, by means of technical skills, of arranging plant materials as they grow naturally (Misho-ryu).

So-no-soe Sō-nō-sō-eh′	Front Earth supplement (Sho-fu-ryu-Moribana).
Subject Stem	Designation applied to Heaven line by Ohara-ryu.
Suiban Sōō-eh-bän′	Basin-type container used for Moribana (and some forms of Informal Ikenobo) arrangements.
Sunabachi sōōn-eh-bä′-chē	Low bronze sand bowl used for certain form of Ikenobo.
Tai Tī	Literal translation: "Material substance." Term applied by most teachers to Earth line in classical forms. Tai is also name of Earth line in Ikenobo-Moribana, and of Heaven branch in Misho-ryu.
Tai-no-mae-zoe Tī-nō-mē-zō-eh′	Front supplement to Heaven in Misho-ryu-Heika.
Tai-no-soe Tī-nō-sō-eh′	Supplement to Heaven in Misho-ryu-Heika.
Tai-no-tome Tī-nō-tō-meh′	Supplement to Heaven in Sho-fu-ryu-Moribana.
Tai-soe Tī-sō-eh′	Heaven supplement in Sho-fu-ryu-Moribana.
Tai-ushiro Tī′-ōō-sē′-rō	Supporting branch in back of Earth (Sho-fu-ryu).
Tani Tä-nē′	"Valley"; lowest group in any Japanese flower arrangement in low, flat container; hides stems of main branches, and flower holders.
Tea Ceremony	An aesthetic ritual concerning subjects not of material nature.
tokonomo tō-kō-nō′-mo	Alcove in a Japanese room.

Tome tō-meh′	Filler (or stopper) in Sho-fu-ryu-Moribana; consists of one or more placements a little behind and to one side of Heaven, always on side opposite to mikoshi. Tome thickens arrangement. (In Misho-ryu classical forms, Earth is designated Tome; and in Misho-ryu Heika, Earth as well as the filler materials are called Tome.)
Tsunagi Sōō-nä′-geh	Supplement to Man (Yu) in Misho-ryu-Moribana, and is called "Relative."
Usubata ōō-sōō-bä′-tä	Traditional container for semi-formal or informal Ikenobo arrangements; has plate-like top section. Bowl and plate may be used together, or as separate containers.
uzumi ōō-zōō-mē′	Short bunches of club moss (we use cypress, lycopodium or the like) to cover stems and pinpoint holders (Sho-fu-ryu-Moribana).
Yo Yō	Man line in Misho-ryu classical forms.
Yu Yōō	Man branch in Misho-ryu-Moribana and Heika.
Yu-no-soe Yōō-nō-so-eh′	Supplement to Man. Made of short bunches of cypress or its equivalent (Misho-ryu-Moribana).

NOTE: Syllables are not accented in Japanese words, but *are* pronounced separately.

REFERENCE MATERIAL

Flowers—East-West, by Gregory Conway (Alfred A. Knopf, Inc., Pub.)

Japanese Flower Arrangement for Modern Homes, by Margaret Preininger (Little, Brown & Co., Boston, Pub.)

Ikenobo School of Japanese Flower Arrangement, compiled by T. Nishimuri, (Rokkaku-Dori, Higashi no Toin, Kyoto, Japan, Pub.)

Japanese Flower Arrangement, by Ellen Gordon Allen (National Council Books Inc., Philadelphia).

Flower Arrangement Art of Japan, by Mary Cokely Wood (Charles E. Tuttle Co., Rutland, Vt. and Tokyo, Japan, 1951, Pub.)

Ikebana—booklet published by Embassy of Japan Information Section, Washington, D. C.

Notes from Classes on Ikenobo School, conducted by Mrs. S. Arai, Houston, Texas.

The Mastery of Japanese Flower Arrangement, by Hein Koshu Tsujii (Mitsubana & Co., Matsugasaki, Kyoto, Japan, Pub.)

Manual of Japanese Flower Arrangement, by Mrs. Josui Oshikawa and Mrs. Hazel Gorham (copyrighted 1936 by Nippon Bunka Remmei, and in 1951 by the Cultural Exchange Club of Tokyo, Japan).

Flower Arrangements of the Ohara School, by Houn Ohara (new edition, Mitsubana & Co., Kyoto, Japan, Pub.)

Ikebana—Souvenir booklet published by Ohara Center, Tokyo, Japan, 1958).

Ikebana—Japanese Flower Arrangements by Sofu Teshigahara—by Sumio Mizusawa, (Sogetsukai, Mita-Tsunamachi Minatoku, Tokyo, Japan, Pub. released in United States by Studio Publications, Inc., New York City)

Ikebana—Sogetsu Flower Arrangement for a Beginner, by Sofu Teshigahari, Pub.)

123

Floral Art of Japan, by Issotei Nishikowa (Maruzen Co., Ltd., Tokyo, 1936. Pub.

"The Theory of Japanese Flower Arrangements," by Josiah Conder, F.R.I.B.A. (Reprint of a paper read by him before the Asiatic Society of Japan, March 13, 1889; published with permission of Asiatic Society of Japan, Tokyo, by J. L. Thompson & Co., Ltd., Kobe Japan, in 1935).

Symbolism in Flower Arrangement by Ervin S. Ferry (The Macmillan Co., 1958).

Index